ALL-ROUND TRAINING FOR THE TOEIC® L&R TEST

Takayuki Ishii / Chinatsu Hirata / Yuko Matsumura
Osamu Yamaguchi / Masahiko Iwata / Joe Ciunci

photographs by
© iStockphoto.com

音声ファイルのダウンロード／ストリーミング

CD マーク表示がある箇所は、音声を弊社 HP より無料でダウンロード／ストリーミングすることができます。トップページのバナーをクリックし、書籍検索してください。書籍詳細ページに音声ダウンロードアイコンがございますのでそちらから自習用音声としてご活用ください。

https://www.seibido.co.jp

ALL-ROUND TRAINING FOR THE TOEIC® L&R TEST
TOEIC®L&R TEST オールラウンド演習

はじめに

TOEIC® L and R TEST については、実に色々なテキストが出版されています。しかし、テキストとしてページ制限がある中で、TOEIC 対策面と英語コミュニケーション教育面の両立や、効率と効果の両面を高める工夫が施されたテキストが、それほど多くはないというのが現状です。

本書はそのような数少ないテキストの1つと言えるでしょう。というのは、本書の特長として、次の5つが挙げられるからです。

●**特長1**　TOEIC 対策の実践面と英語能力養成の教育面を両立させている。TOEIC の範囲を超える語彙・語法・文法も扱う場合がありますが、これは英語能力向上を目的とする教育において必要だからです。

●**特長2**　全ての Part において、Phase 1 と Phase 2 の段階性を設けている。
Phase 1 で基礎的な練習問題、その後、Phase 2 で実践的な練習問題を提示しています。

●**特長3**　各章はトピック別の構成で、全ての Part に様々なテーマを設けている。全14章に総合テーマがあり、各 Part にそれぞれの個別テーマが設けられ、そのテーマに基づく問題を提示しています。

●**特長4**　コラムは語彙・語法・文法・TOEIC 対策などがあり、充実している。
TOEIC 語彙・語法と文法のコラムは全章共通、語彙チェックと語法チェック、そして、各 Part の攻略法のコラムは、必要に応じて添えています。

●**特長5**　Listening Section と Reading Section の設問数が豊富にある。
Listening の設問数は15問、Reading Section の設問数は14～16問、Phase 1 については、Listening において16問、Reading において12問となっています。

本書の執筆においては、平田が Part 1 および Part 6 の後半、松村が Part 2 と Part 5、山口が Part 3 と Part 4 および Part 6 の前半、岩田が Part 7、Ciunci が全体の校閲、石井が1章と12章全体と、全章の PreTOEIC Section とコラム、そして全体の監修を担当しました。

また、本書を製作するにあたり、有益な助言と励ましをいただきました成美堂の田村栄一氏、更に、編集の細部にわたり、いろいろとお世話いただきました佐野泰一氏には、心から感謝の意を表したいと思います。

本書を通して、TOEIC テストのスコアの向上と共に、英語コミュニケーション能力の涵養に、少しでも貢献できれば、著者としてこれ以上の喜びはありません。

石井　隆之
著者代表

本書の構成とテーマ

■ 1 章の頁構成（標準パターン）

1 ページ目

章タイトル
Pre-TOEIC Section
●語彙チェック
● TOEIC
語彙と語法

2 ページ目

Listening Section
★ Part 1
◎ Phase 1
◎ Phase 2
必要に応じコラム
があり

3 ページ目

★ Part 2
◎ Phase 1
◎ Phase 2
★ Part 3
◎ Phase 1

4 ページ目

◎ Phase 2
必要に応じコラム
があり

5 ページ目

★ Part 4
◎ Phase 1
◎ Phase 2
必要に応じコラム
があり

6 ページ目

Reading Section
★ Part 5
◎ Phase 1
◎ Phase 2

7 ページ目

●文法チェック
★ Part 6
◎ Phase 1
必要に応じコラム
があり

8 ページ目

◎ Phase 2
必要に応じコラム
があり

9 ページ目

★ Part 7
◎ Phase 1
◎ Phase 2
※ Part 7 のページ数
は 2～3 ページ

各章のPart別・個別テーマ

●リスニングセクション

章	Part 2	Part 3	Part 4
1	What	Whichの設問(図表)	親会の予定（図表）
2	Who	Whatの設問（3人）	特別セールのお知らせ
3	Which	Whoの設問	忘れ物に関する記事
4	Where	Whyの設問（3人）	列車遅延のニュース
5	When	How＋形容詞/副詞の設問	記念切手の配布（図表）
6	Why	Whereの設問	新金融商品の案内
7	How	前置詞+Whichの設問（図表）	空港でのアナウンス
8	How＋形容詞/副詞	人間関係を問う（3人）	ホテル朝食会場（図表）
9	Yes / No形式	問題点を問う	講演する医師の紹介
10	Orの入った疑問	職業を問う	会社説明会の案内
11	付加疑問文	提案を問う	学会のプログラム案内
12	提案/勧誘の文	行動を問う（3人＋意図）	会社の沿革の挨拶（図表）
13	依頼/許可の文	会話の場所を問う	出張計画のスピーチ
14	意外な応答	最も～なのは？を問う	名所の説明のスピーチ

●リーディングセクション

章	Part 5	Part 6	Part 7
1	動詞の時制	ケータリング	メニュー＋Ｅメール２つ
2	自動詞と他動詞	迷子のお知らせ	Ｅメール１つ＋広告
3	主語と動詞の一致	地下鉄の駅への道案内	Ｅメール１つ
4	動名詞	美術館への道案内	ビジネスレター１つ
5	不定詞	日本の切手の歴史	SNS 問題（１）
6	副詞	銀行の合併後の案内	SNS 問題（２）
7	分詞	到着ロビーの説明	Ｅメール１つ
8	名詞の可算・不可算	ホテルでの注意事項	ニュース（文の位置問題）
9	代名詞	健康診断での諸注意	ニュース
10	接続詞と接続副詞	イベント会場の手配	Ｅメール２つ
11	受動態と使役	大学の留学プログラム	Ｅメール２つ＋講座案内
12	関係詞	予定変更依頼のメール	案内通知＋Ｅメール１つ
13	形容詞	ホテル推薦のメール	Ｅメール３つ
14	前置詞	観光ツアーの案内文	Ｅメール２つ＋添付資料

CONTENTS

UNIT 1

Restaurant

PRE-TOEIC SECTION

Vocabulary Check

次の (1) から (10) の英単語が当てはまる英文を下の (a) ～ (j) から選びなさい。

(1) boom (　　)　**(2)** contain (　　)　**(3)** detail (　　)　**(4)** hike (　　)
(5) ingredient (　　)　**(6)** lower (　　)　**(7)** manager (　　)
(8) organize (　　)　**(9)** recommend (　　)　**(10)** summarize (　　)

(a) I (　　) that Jack study more about Japanese culture.
(b) A poor diet (　　)-ed her vitality.
(c) He finally had to (　　) the long story.
(d) Every (　　) of Mary's report was perfect.
(e) By the 2010's, the smartphone industry was (　　)-ing.
(f) Salt is an essential (　　) in cooking.
(g) The sales (　　) decided to hold an urgent sales meeting.
(h) I am going to (　　) the schedule for the business trip.
(i) The union is pressing for a five-percent pay (　　).
(j) The pitcher (　　)-ed enough milk for all of them.

TOEIC 語彙と語法 1　**多義語 order**

① 「順序」 in numerical order (番号順に) / in ascending order (低い順に)
② 「調子」 in bad order (不調で) / keep it in good order (整頓しておく)
③ 「秩序」 keep order (秩序を守る) / disturb law and order (治安を乱す)
④ 「命令」 obey orders (命令に従う) / give orders (命令を下す)
⑤ 「注文」 give an order for A to B (A を B に注文する) [=place an order with B for A]
⑥ 「為替」 exchange order (為替手形) [=draft; bill of exchange]
⑦ 「階層」 all orders of society (社会の全階層の人たち)
⑧ 「勲章」 the Order of Cultural Merit (文化勲章) [=Cultural Medal]

LISTENING SECTION

Part 1 写真描写問題

Phase 1 Listen to the following statements and fill in the blanks.  1-02

1.

Ⓐ Ⓑ Ⓒ Ⓓ

(A) They're eating ( ).

(B) They're ( ) the menu.

(C) They're going ( ) of the restaurant.

(D) They're looking ( ) each other.

Phase 2 1-03、04

2.

Ⓐ Ⓑ Ⓒ Ⓓ

3.

Ⓐ Ⓑ Ⓒ Ⓓ

Part 2 応答問題

Phase 1 Listen, fill in the blank and choose the best response.

CD 1-05、06

4. What did you eat (   ) your lunch?
   (A)(   ) a hamburger today.
   (B) Yes, you're (   ).
   (C) I ate (   ) yesterday.

5. What's (   ) recommendation?
   (A) This is (   ) recommendation.
   (B) You (   ) it.
   (C) Well, (   ) me think.

Phase 2

CD 1-07、08、09、10

6. Mark your answer on your answer sheet. Ⓐ Ⓑ Ⓒ

7. Mark your answer on your answer sheet. Ⓐ Ⓑ Ⓒ

8. Mark your answer on your answer sheet. Ⓐ Ⓑ Ⓒ

9. Mark your answer on your answer sheet. Ⓐ Ⓑ Ⓒ

Part 3 会話問題

Phase 1 Choose the better word that suits the blank.

(a) May I (make / take) your order?
(b) This (costs / prices) more than I expected.
(c) She is concerned (about / with) her weight; therefore, she is on a diet.
(d) What's (on / in) the menu today?---Today's special is grilled salmon.

Phase 2

Burger		Drink	S	M	L
· Special Hamburger	$6.00	· Coffee	$1.00	$1.50	$1.75
· Giant Cheeseburger	$5.00	· Smoothie	$3.00	$3.50	$4.00
· Cheeseburger	$4.50	(Strawberry, Mango)			
· Special Fish Burger	$5.50				
· Vegetable Burger	$4.00				

10. Why does the woman change her order?
(A) She is concerned about her weight.
(B) She is a vegetarian.
(C) She is hungry after hiking.
(D) She is surprised to see a price increase.

11. Look at the graphic. What is the price of the burger the woman will eat?
(A) $4.00
(B) $4.50
(C) $5.00
(D) $5.50

12. Which is NOT contained in the vegetable burger?
(A) Avocado
(B) Chopped cabbage
(C) Sliced onion
(D) Lettuce

Part 4 説明文問題

Phase 1 Fill in the blank with the most appropriate word.

(a) Thank you (   ) e-mailing me about your current situation.
(b) The annual conference will be held (   ) March 24 next year.
(c) I got an urgent e-mail just (   ) few minutes ago.
(d) It is (   ) what we should do but how we should do it that counts.

Phase 2

	Tom	Joe	Bob	Lucy	Elizabeth
Dec. 18	○	×	×	○	×
Dec. 19	○	○	×	×	○
Dec. 20	○	○	×	○	○
Dec. 21	○	○	○	○	○

Mark the days on which you are available with a circle. If you are not, put an "X."

13. Why did Elizabeth call the speaker?
(A) To ask when the get-together is going to be held
(B) To recommend he choose a Chinese restaurant for the meeting
(C) To tell him to book a French restaurant for the get-together
(D) To inform him about a change in her availability

14. Look at the graphic. Which day did the speaker finally decide on for the get-together?
(A) Dec. 18 (B) Dec. 19 (C) Dec. 20 (D) Dec. 21

15. With which people were Bob and Lucy supposed to have a sales meeting?
(A) Japanese (B) Chinese (C) Italians (D) Frenchmen

Part 4 対処法 ① 図表とリスニングの両方に集中する

図表入りの Part 4 問題に、その図表を見て答える設問が必ずあるが、リスニング内容を理解しないと解けない問題となっている。設問の図を見て選択肢を読むだけでは不十分であるので、注意しよう！

語法チェック about と「心配」のニュアンス

(1) concerned about ～：～について心配している
concerned with ～：～に関わる、関係している、関心がある
(2) anxious about ～：～について心配している
anxious for ～：～を強く求めている
(3) care about ～：～のことを心配する、～のことを気にする
care for ～：～のことが好きである、～の面倒を見る、～をいたわる

READING SECTION

Part 5 短文穴埋問題

Phase 1 Choose the better word or phrase that suits the blank.

1. I (study / am studying) English for three hours every Saturday.
2. When (have you / did you) arrive in Japan?---About a week ago.
3. The manager (works / will work) on the project until tomorrow morning.

Phase 2

4. We ------- to the mom-and-pop candy store together to buy the snacks.
(A) used to go
(B) were used to go
(C) used going
(D) used to going

5. Our job ------- very easy to handle since our company's president introduced the new computer system.
(A) makes
(B) is making
(C) has made
(D) has been made

6. The explorer was thought to ------- but he has returned alive and well.
(A) disappear
(B) be disappearing
(C) have disappeared
(D) be disappeared

7. Nancy ------- her daughter out of taking part in the dangerous expedition.
(A) said
(B) told
(C) talked
(D) spoke

文法チェック **動詞の時制**

●重要法則・・・時制の確認は副詞が決め手

yesterday, ~years ago など過去を表す副詞があれば、その文の動詞の時制は過去形にしなければならない。

before（以前に）、~times（～回）、ever や never などがあれば、完了形 (have ＋過去分詞) の時制で、経験を表す。

for ~ days（～日間）や since（～以来）などの句が来ると、同じ完了形でも継続を表す。

●重要法則・・・前置詞に注意する

例えば、in ~ minutes（～分後）は「現在から～分経てば」の意味である。未来時制と共に用いる。→ I will be back in ten minutes.（10 分後に戻ります）

注：after 10 minutes とは言わない。

Part 6 長文穴埋問題

Phase 1 Choose the best word or phrase that suits the blank.

(a) That sounds exciting, so let me give (it / one / them) a try.

(b) The difficult tasks proceeded without a (hatch / hitch / hutch).

(c) He is 70, give (and / but / or) take a few years.

(d) I don’t like to leave things up in the (air / sky / wind).

Phase 2

Dear John,

I'm going to give the catering company a -------(8.) this afternoon. It's my responsibility to organize this year's summer cookout at our main office. -------(9.) Therefore, I hope this one can also go off without a hitch. I'll keep my fingers crossed. This year we'll be successful because we've already got at least -------(10.) people expected to attend with a possible 70 in total, give or take. I'm going to order enough so that we can accommodate everyone if all decide to come. I've decided to order French fries and cheese sticks as well as some spare ribs. The plan is still up in the air as to -------(11.) I should order the seafood platter or fried chicken. I've settled on soda and water for drinks. Any ideas or requests?

Thanks,

Nancy

8. (A) boil (B) call (C) tilt (D) try

9. (A) Fortunately, last year's sales meeting was successful.
(B) Unfortunately, the last year's party was cancelled.
(C) Last year's event was a complete disaster.
(D) Last year's party was a great success.

10. (A) 50 (B) 70 (C) 80 (D) 90

11. (A) if (B) in which (C) what (D) whether or not

Part 6 対処法 ① 前後の文を読む

空所は、空所のある文だけではなく、その前後を見ないと適切なものが分からない場合が多い。なお、適切な文を選ぶ設問が必ず１つあり、その場合は、まさに、前後の文を読み、つじつまが合う文を選択する。

Part 7 読解問題

Phase 1 Choose the best word or phrase that suits the blank.

(a) We are (searching / searching for / seeking) franchisees.
(b) I am thinking of making a (career / carrier / courier) change.
(c) She always orders (lamb steak / ram stake / rum steak) dinner.
(d) He signed the agreement to kick (in / off / on) the new business.
(e) The applicant has to (attend / attend to / attend on) the training session.

Phase 2

Charley's Steak House Seattle, Newly Opened

Great Food & Great Location

Menu:
-Sirloin steak with fresh vegetables ⇒ $30
-16 oz T-Bone steak with fresh vegetables ⇒ $25
-Lamb steak with a cup of garlic and onion soup ⇒ $20
*Garlic rice or bread is served at an additional charge of $1.50

Every guest can enjoy dining in a cozy atmosphere with a great ocean view.

P.S. We are seeking franchisees all over the country. If you are interested, please contact us by e-mail anytime.
E-mail address: charleysteak@orange.com
Owner, Charley Simpson

Dear Charley Simpson,
This e-mail is in response to the advertisement for your steak house that you put on the Internet. I am David MacArthur, living in downtown, Chicago. Since graduating from a state university, I have been working for a reputable sporting goods company with the world's most popular baseball uniform brand.
However, I am interested in making a career change. I would like to start a new business immediately, if possible. As you may know, the sporting goods industry has not been booming for years. I often eat at your restaurant and I always order the lamb steak dinner with garlic rice. So, I would appreciate it if you could give me more details on how to become a franchisee for a Charley's restaurant.

I am looking forward to hearing from you soon.

Best regards,
David MacArthur

Dear David MacArthur,

Thank you very much for your interest in our steak house. I am very pleased to give you more details about running a franchise.
Requirements for a franchisee:
One-time initial fee: $50,000
Royalty: 8% of monthly sales
Attendance at a three-month training course

The training allows a franchisee to learn about site selection, operating manuals, brand standards, quality controls and marketing strategies. Before you attend a training session, you need to sign a franchise agreement for kicking off the steak house business.

I am looking forward to your reply.

Best regards,

Charley Simpson
Owner, Charley's Steak House

12. Why was the advertisement posted on the Internet?
(A) To let people know more about the restaurant
(B) To seek applicants for a franchise
(C) To advertise a new menu item
(D) To inform customers of the restaurant's relocation

13. Why did Mr. MacArthur e-mail Mr. Simpson?
(A) He wants to start a sporting goods-related business.
(B) He has to find a new job because he is unemployed.
(C) He wants to change his job as soon as possible.
(D) He has to ask another person to be a franchisee.

14. What is the price of the dish the applicant regularly orders?
(A) $20 (B) $21.50 (C) $26.50 (D) $31.50

15. What is a franchisee probably unable to learn at a training session?
(A) Specific information about the fast food industry
(B) How to operate a restaurant
(C) Quality control techniques
(D) Marketing strategies for a franchise

16. Which of the following descriptions is correct?
(A) The company David works for is not reputable at all.
(B) Mr. Simpson thinks the sporting goods industry is unpopular nowadays.
(C) The training session will last for three months.
(D) An applicant has to attend a training session before signing a contract.

Part 7 **対処法 ① triple passage 問題は 5 つの設問**

1つの問題に対して、設問が最高で5つある。double passage 問題と triple passage 問題に対しては必ず5設問。設問を先に読むと速く解答できる。

語法チェック **I would appreciate it if you could …**
(…して頂ければ光栄です)

appreciate には「評価する、鑑賞する、的確に認識する、値上がりする」などの意味があるが、ビジネス文で、I would appreciate it if …の構造が重要である。it は、if 以下の状況を漠然と指す目的語であるが、これを省略できない点に注意する。

UNIT 2 Department Store

PRE-TOEIC SECTION

Vocabulary Check

次の (1) から (10) の英単語が当てはまる英文を下の (a) 〜 (j) から選びなさい。

(1) appreciate (　　) **(2)** backpack (　　) **(3)** discount (　　) **(4)** install (　　)
(5) mention (　　) **(6)** refund (　　) **(7)** reimburse (　　)
(8) relocation (　　) **(9)** retailer (　　) **(10)** subordinate (　　)

(a) The expert workers (　　)ed a heating system in my house.
(b) Please return your purchase to the (　　) if it breaks down.
(c) You can get a (　　) on the ticket if the train is over two hours late.
(d) I would (　　) it if you could send me an illustrated catalogue.
(e) We will allow a 10-percent (　　) off list prices.
(f) The boss made an incisive comment to his (　　).
(g) He had all his possessions in a (　　) while traveling around the world.
(h) Our company's (　　) site has yet to be decided.
(i) I have something very important to (　　) in this connection.
(j) If you pay for the repair now, the insurance company will (　　) you later.

TOEIC 語彙と語法 2 客のいろいろ

① guest 招待客、ホテルの客
② customer 店やレストランの客、顧客、取引先、得意先
③ client 顧客、（弁護士などの）依頼人
④ shopper 買い物客
⑤ sightseer 観光客
⑥ tourist 旅行客、観光客、遠征中のスポーツ選手
⑦ spectator スポーツなどの観客 cf. 劇場などの客 audience
⑧ passenger 乗客
⑨ visitor 訪問客 (=caller)

LISTENING SECTION

Part 1 写真描写問題

Phase 1 Listen to the following statements and fill in the blanks.  1-15

1.

Ⓐ Ⓑ Ⓒ Ⓓ

(A) The woman is ( ) cloth bags.

(B) The woman is ( ) paper bags in both hands.

(C) The woman is buying something at a department ( ).

(D) The woman is wearing a ( ) gown.

Phase 2 1-16、17

2.

Ⓐ Ⓑ Ⓒ Ⓓ

3.

Ⓐ Ⓑ Ⓒ Ⓓ

Part 2 応答問題

Phase 1 Listen, fill in the blank and choose the best response. CD 1-18、19

4. Who would you like to go ( ) with?
   (A) With one of my ( ).
   (B) I like going shopping on ( ).
   (C) To department stores in the downtown ( ).

5. What ( ) are you looking for?
   (A) I'm looking for a position in a ( ) company.
   (B) I'm looking ( ) to hearing from you.
   (C) Any of the top Italian ( ) brands.

Phase 2 CD 1-20、21、22、23

6. Mark your answer on your answer sheet. Ⓐ Ⓑ Ⓒ
7. Mark your answer on your answer sheet. Ⓐ Ⓑ Ⓒ
8. Mark your answer on your answer sheet. Ⓐ Ⓑ Ⓒ
9. Mark your answer on your answer sheet. Ⓐ Ⓑ Ⓒ

Part 2 対処法 ① 問いかけ文をしっかり聞く

問いかけ文に出てくる単語や表現を用いた選択肢は答えでないことが多い。

Part 3 会話問題

Phase 1 Choose the better word that suits the blank.

(a) I know something has been (up / down) with you for the past few years.
(b) I am just (wandering / wondering) if you could give me a helping hand.
(c) I think you need to (get / take) in touch with the person in charge.
(d) Thank you for (reminding / remembering) me to mail the letter.

Phase 2

10. How long has the supplier provided service to the company?
(A) A year
(B) Over one year
(C) Six months
(D) Two weeks

11. What is the problem?
(A) The supplier cancelled the order.
(B) The supplier forgot to deliver the goods.
(C) The goods were delivered late.
(D) The trading company went bankrupt.

12. What is most likely the relationship between Roy and the women?
(A) He is their colleague.
(B) He is subordinate to them.
(C) He is their boss.
(D) He is their customer.

Part 3 対処法 ①

必ず1つの会話に対し３設問があるので、あらかじめ3つの設問を読んでおく。すると、どういうところに注意して会話を聞けばよいのかが分かる。

Part 4 説明文問題

Phase 1 **Fill in the blank with the most appropriate word.**

(a) The flight was delayed due (   ) trouble with the plane.
(b) This system will be introduced as (   ) February 22, 2022.
(c) I would appreciate (   ) if you could tackle the problem.
(d) These electric appliances will be available for 10 percent (   ) the regular price.

Phase 2

13. When will the market shorten its business hours?
(A) April 30
(B) May 1
(C) August 1
(D) The middle of the month

14. What is planned in mid-August?
(A) The renovation of the parking lot
(B) A bargain sale
(C) The relocation of the store
(D) Shutting up shop

15. Who can benefit most from the 20 percent discount offered?
(A) Any customer with a membership card
(B) Customers having free parking tickets
(C) Customers buying fresh vegetables
(D) Any customer shopping on weekends

READING SECTION

Part 5 短文穴埋問題

Phase 1 Choose the better word or phrase that suits the blank.

1. Let's (discuss / discuss about) sales strategies for the next quarter together.
2. He (mentioned / mentioned about) the theory behind the marketing strategies he came up with.
3. Will you (attend / attend at) the opening ceremony for the flagship store?

Phase 2

4. I can't ------- the way the store clerks deal with shoppers anymore.
(A) consider
(B) find
(C) stand
(D) run

5. The sales in the distribution company have ------- sharply in recent years.
(A) raise
(B) raised
(C) rise
(D) risen

6. The businessperson ------- this department store as well as other retail outlets.
(A) walks
(B) retires
(C) runs
(D) sells

7. The customer ------- to the sales clerk about the defective shirt he had bought at the department store.
(A) apologized
(B) claimed
(C) complained
(D) told

文法チェック **自動詞と他動詞**

●重要法則・・・自動詞と間違えやすい他動詞は、日本語の助詞に注意する
「と」は with、「に」は to や into、「について」は about でない。
彼女と結婚する⇒ marry her (× marry with her)
父親に似ている⇒ resemble one's father（× resemble to one's father)
そのビルに入る⇒ enter the building（× enter into the building)
その問題について触れる⇒ mention the problem (× mention about the problem)

●重要法則・・・他動詞と間違えやすい自動詞は、前置詞に注意する
～に・・・のことで謝る⇒ apologize to ～ for・・・
～に答える⇒ reply to ～ 注：answer は to が不要。answer ～
～に反対する⇒ object to ～ 注：oppose は to が不要。oppose ～
～に取りかかる⇒ attend to one's duties（仕事に取りかかる）
注：前置詞なしの attend ～は「～に出席する」

Part 6 長文穴埋問題

Phase 1 Choose the best word or phrase that suits the blank.

(a) I found (little boy / a little boy / little boys) named Bob crying on the street.
(b) She looked around in the women's wear (corner / section / place) in the store.
(c) The man was wearing a T-shirt with the words Great Man (at / on / in) it.
(d) I heard my close friend Susan (sing / sung / to sing) a solo at the concert.

Phase 2

Your attention, please. We have a little boy named Roy. He was -------- (8.) in the vegetable section -------- (9.) the first floor. He is wearing an ocean-blue T-shirt, white shorts and a cap with the words *New York* across the front. He also has on a backpack with *Tokyo Olympics 2020* on it. He is around five years old and was heard crying for his mother. -------- (10.) We have him here at the information counter on the first floor. Come see Ms. Sanchez at the counter if you have any information. Thank you very much for your -------- (11.) .

8. (A) founded
(B) found
(C) finding
(D) finds

9. (A) at　　(B) of
(C) on　　(D) off

10. (A) Is there anyone who knows who this boy is?
(B) Is there anything known about his mother?
(C) Is there anything this boy knows?
(D) Is there anyone whose mother is looking for him?

11. (A) action
(B) appreciation
(C) advantage
(D) attention

Part 6　**対処法 ②　論理性もチェックする**

Part 5 は文法や語彙のチェックを中心とするが、Part 6 はまとまったパッセージ内での文法や語彙チェック以外に、語法なども含め、何より、文章の流れの中で、最も適切な文を選ぶ問題がある。これは、文の展開上、一番論理的な文はどれかを選ばせる問題が特徴である。つまり、常に文の流れを追っておく必要がある。

Part 7 読解問題

Phase 1 Choose the best word or phrase that suits the blank.

(a) Most (kitchen wear / kitchen ware / kitchen waste) is on sale this weekend.
(b) Let's take a walk with the (baby car / baby carriage / baby chair) for a while.
(c) The new equipment will be (intended / installed / imposed) in our factory this weekend.
(d) Please (make / take / watch) sure that all doors are locked.
(e) I would appreciate it (whether / that / if) you could join us.

Phase 2

To: inquiry@AdamsDepartment.com
From: j.oliver@coolmail.com
Date: January 21
Subject: Recall

Dear Sir or Madam,

I saw your recall notice in the newspaper this morning and would like to verify whether my case will be covered or not. Currently, my stroller does not seem to have the parts in question, because the attachment cracked and I was unable to use the stroller. I threw the attachment away about a year ago, although I still own the hood itself.

As my daughter really likes the stroller, I would prefer to have a new one rather than get a full refund. I would appreciate it if you could inform me whether the free replacement offer is applicable to my case or not. Also, please let me know if I can purchase the latest model by paying the difference, if that's what it takes.

Looking forward to hearing from you.
Best regards,

Jim Oliver
438-897-3362(mobile)
336 Hay Street, North Valley, CA 90210

Product Safety Recall by O'Neal Baby's Ware Pty Ltd

- Product Name: Snail Stroller
- Product No: All batches
- Product Description: N-series with a big red hood
- Defect: Incorrect installation of the small attachment between the stroller and hood.
- Hazard: Small parts of the products could potentially come off, presenting a choking hazard.
- What To Do: Consumers should immediately refrain from using the stroller and return it to the retailer for a full refund or contact our local representatives to set up an appointment to replace the parts free of charge.

12. What product is being recalled?
(A) Baby clothes (B) Baby carriages (C) Baby toys (D) Baby parasols

13. Where should a consumer bring the stroller if they want to be reimbursed?
(A) To a local representative (B) To the maker that produced the item
(C) To an insurance company (D) To the shop where the purchase was made

14. What does Jim Oliver most likely want to have replaced?
(A) Parts at issue (B) The attachment (C) The stroller (D) The hood

15. What problem does Jim Oliver mention in his e-mail?
(A) He damaged the hood itself. (B) He discarded the stroller.
(C) He doesn't have all the parts. (D) He couldn't get a refund.

16. What will Jim Oliver most likely do if the difference quoted is small?
(A) He will keep the product. (B) He will demand a refund.
(C) He will have the product fixed. (D) He will purchase the newest model.

語法チェック　「無料で」という表現

free of charge (=without charge) 以外に、for free も使える。他に gratis もある。
⇒ You can park here free of charge. [=…for free.]（駐車料金は不要です）
This sample is gratis.（このサンプルは無料です）

UNIT 3 Train Station

PRE-TOEIC SECTION

Vocabulary Check

次の (1) から (10) の英単語が当てはまる英文を下の (a) ～ (j) から選びなさい。

(1) bound (　　) **(2)** compensation (　　) **(3)** delay (　　) **(4)** financial (　　)
(5) incur (　　) **(6)** postpone (　　) **(7)** rank (　　) **(8)** result (　　)
(9) valid (　　) **(10)** vicinity (　　)

(a) Refrain from doing anything that may (　　) suspicion.
(b) I paid 500,000 yen in (　　) for the injury.
(c) These quotes are (　　) for 15 days.
(d) I am very sorry for the (　　) in my reply.
(e) Our company (　　)s third in sales volume among the companies in this field.
(f) Mary decided that she would (　　) her departure.
(g) She may have missed the train (　　) for London.
(h) This animal inhabits the area in the (　　) of a river.
(i) Our president's plan (　　)ed in great success.
(j) The nation has been in (　　) difficulties for about a decade.

TOEIC 語彙と語法 3　予約や予定に関する表現

① 予約する　book; reserve; make a booking; make a reservation
② 仮予約する（仮押さえする）make a tentative reservation
③ 再度予約する、予約し直す rebook
④ 予約（予定や注文）をキャンセルする　cancel
cancel a hotel reservation（ホテルの予約をキャンセルする）
cancel an order（注文をキャンセルする）
⑤ 予定をする、スケジュールを組む　schedule ～; plan for ～
schedule a concert（コンサートを予定する）
⑥ スケジュールを組み直す reschedule

LISTENING SECTION

Part 1 写真描写問題

Phase 1 Listen to the following statements and fill in the blanks.  1-28

1.

Ⓐ Ⓑ Ⓒ Ⓓ

(A) The train has not ( ) at the station yet.

(B) ( ) are coming out of the train.

(C) Wheelchair-( ) people can use the train.

(D) Everyone ( ) is entering the train.

Phase 2 1-29、30

2.

Ⓐ Ⓑ Ⓒ Ⓓ

3.

Ⓐ Ⓑ Ⓒ Ⓓ

Part 1

対処法① 人と物に着目する

人が写っている場合は、何をしているかと、どんな服装をしているかに着目し、物が複数写っている場合は、その位置関係に着目しておこう。

Part 2 応答問題

Phase 1 Listen, fill in the blank and choose the best response. CD 1-31、32

4. Which platform does the express train (   ) from?
(A) Number three, if I remember (   ).
(B) The train will depart (   ).
(C) Please (   ) for me on the platform.

5. Which train should I change (   )?
(A) (   ) Shibuya Station.
(B) The one (   ) for Shinjuku.
(C) All (   ) are listed alphabetically.

Phase 2 CD 1-33、34、35、36

6. Mark your answer on your answer sheet. Ⓐ Ⓑ Ⓒ

7. Mark your answer on your answer sheet. Ⓐ Ⓑ Ⓒ

8. Mark your answer on your answer sheet. Ⓐ Ⓑ Ⓒ

9. Mark your answer on your answer sheet. Ⓐ Ⓑ Ⓒ

Part 3 会話問題

Phase 1 Choose the better word that suits the blank.

(a) He often (falls / feels) behind in his bills.
(b) We are busy because our company is (overstaffed / understaffed).
(c) All the (personal / personnel) will be given an extra week's vacation.
(d) Let me tell you (what / how) I can do to help you deal with the problem.

Phase 2

10. Who is supposed to get a financial report?
(A) Mary
(B) John
(C) The accounting department
(D) The president

11. What is the woman's problem?
(A) She was severely sick for a few weeks.
(B) She took a business trip.
(C) Her department is short of workers.
(D) Her staff lost some summaries.

12. What will John try to do for Mary?
(A) Write a financial report
(B) Transfer to her office to help her
(C) Request assistance from upper management
(D) Rewrite the summaries

Part 4 説明文問題

Phase 1 Fill in the blank with the most appropriate word.

(a) (   ) of the major problems we face at present is a financial one.
(b) We have to deal (   ) the demanding customer in some way or other.
(c) You should quickly go to a lost and (   ) counter at the station.
(d) (   ) time it takes to complete this task may be more than one month.

Phase 2

CD 1-39、40

13. Which is the most troublesome for staff at railway stations?
(A) Stolen items (B) Quarrels (C) Drunk people (D) Lost umbrellas

14. Which items are NOT mentioned as ones that are left on the train?
(A) Passports (B) Books (C) Raingear (D) Smartphones

15. Which is said to be found in the purse left on the train?
(A) A lot of money (B) medicine for headaches
(C) Various receipts (D) A commuter ticket

語法チェック **staff の用法**

可算名詞の用法で、不定冠詞とともに用いる場合
⇒ a staff of twenty people（20 名の職員）
可算名詞の用法であるが、常に複数扱いで用いる場合
⇒ 20 staff（20 人のスタッフたち）
※「彼は…のスタッフだ」の表現に注意。
⇒× He is a staff of…
○ He is on the staff of …
○ He is a staff member of …

READING SECTION

Part 5 短文穴埋問題

Phase 1 Choose the better word that suits the blank.

1. Mary as well as her sisters (is / are) a commuter on the train.
2. Either one of us (is / are) going to buy a round-trip ticket.
3. (Has / Have) police already arrived at the site of the accident?

Phase 2

4. The number of passengers who use the bullet train ------- increased sharply in recent years.
(A) has
(B) had
(C) have
(D) will

5. A large number of passengers always ------- on and off at Tokyo Station.
(A) get
(B) gets
(C) is gotten
(D) has gotten

6. Waiting three hours for the delayed train ------- truly exhausting yesterday.
(A) is
(B) are
(C) was
(D) were

7. Neither a limited express train nor semi-express trains ------- been delayed despite the stormy weather.
(A) has
(B) having
(C) have
(D) will

文法チェック　主語と動詞の一致

●重要法則・・・次の表現では動詞に近い方の名詞句 (= B) の数に合わせる
either A or B、neither A nor B、not only A but also B
注：A as well as B では A の数に合わせる。

●重要法則・・・number の表現に注意する
A number of ～ s are ···.（多くの数の～が ··· だ）
The number of ～ s is ···.（～の数は ··· だ）
参考：a number of cars（多くの車）、the number of cars（車の数）、the number of the car（その車のナンバー）

Part 5　対処法 ①　空所内に入る適切な形を考える

動詞句が入る場合は、時制が適切か、自動詞と他動詞のどちらが適切か、能動態と受動態のどちらが適切か、全て適切なら、最後に語法は適切かを考える。

Part 6 長文穴埋問題

Phase 1 Choose the best word or phrase that suits the blank.

(a) There is a large bookstore in the (locality / calamity / vicinity) of the school.
(b) The post office is not so (far / free / away) from the city hall.
(c) I often go shopping at the (drag / drug / drip) store in front of the station.
(d) Keep (to walk / walked / walking) to the next intersection, and you will find it.

Phase 2

The Subway Station

In fact, there are two subway stations in the vicinity of our office building. The subway you have asked me about is not so far from our workplace. -------- **8.** , just exit on the street level of this building we work -------- **9.** and turn right, but be careful of traffic. Keep walking straight for four blocks -------- **10.** you come to a drug store at the corner. You'll also see an ABC convenience store across the street. Turn left at the corner and keep walking to the third traffic light. On the way to the light, you will pass another convenience store on your left. You'll find the large department store on your left. -------- **11.** .

8. (A) In the end
(B) First of all
(C) Furthermore
(D) On the contrary

9. (A) on (B) at
(C) off (D) out

10. (A) lest (B) by
(C) unless (D) until

11. (A) The bus terminal you are looking for is next to it.
(B) The drug store is just around the corner from the department store.
(C) The subway station is just in front of the department store, across the street.
(D) The ABC convenience store is just in the front of the department store.

語法チェック **the のあるなしで意味と語法が異なるものがある**

(1) in front of the room（その部屋の前で / に）
in the front of the room（その部屋の前の方で / に）[部屋の中の前の方を意味]
(2) A is in charge of B. [=B is in the charge of A]（A は B を担当している）
(3) A is in possession of B. [=B is in A's possession.]（A は B を所有している）

Part 7 読解問題

Phase 1 Choose the best word that suits the blank.

(a) The insurance company rejected the (class / clay / claim) for damages.
(b) He boarded a train (bond / bound / bounded) for Berlin.
(c) We are compelled (to / for / in) obey the order.
(d) The event will be postponed (on / in / to) case of rain.
(e) (Confirmation / Consumption / Compensation) often refers to money.

Phase 2

To: inquiry@nationalrailwayservice.com
From: h.benson@freemail.com <Harry Benson>
Date: 11 October
Subject: Claim for compensation

Dear Customer Service,
With this letter I would like to request compensation according to National Railway Regulation Section 3 for the amount of $25.
On 24th September, train 789 bound for South Bank departing from Canterbury was delayed for more than two hours without any reasons given. This caused me to miss the connecting train from South Bank to Table Valley. In order to book a seat on a later train to Table Valley, I was asked to pay an additional incurred charge of $25.
According to National Railway Regulation Section 3, in case of delays without accompanying reasons that result in missing a transfer, National Railway is supposed to fully compensate passengers who have been inconvenienced. I confirmed your regulations with station staff at Huffington Station today.
I have attached files of scanned receipts and tickets to prove my claim. Please send me the above-mentioned sum as soon as possible after receipt of this letter to the bank account below.
I look forward to your reply.
Yours sincerely,

Harry Benson

12. Which of the following statements is true about Harry Benson?
(A) He boarded train 789 from South Bank.
(B) He filled out the required documents for a refund.
(C) He got a refund at Huffington Station.
(D) He was compelled to pay to rebook a seat.

13. Which station did Harry Benson finally arrive at on September 24?
(A) South Bank
(B) Canterbury
(C) Table Valley
(D) Huffington

14. When did Harry Benson most likely confirm the regulations?
(A) Sept. 11
(B) Sept. 24
(C) Oct. 11
(D) Oct. 24

15. Why did Harry Benson send this e-mail?
(A) To complain about services
(B) To get his money back
(C) To ask how to change trains
(D) To get a refund of all fares

語彙チェック　「乗る」と「降りる」の表現

大きな乗り物の乗り降りは、on と off を用いる。
get on a bus（バスに乗る）、get on a train（列車に乗る）
get on a plane（飛行機に乗る）[= board a plane]
get off a bus（バスから降りる）、get off a train（列車から降りる）
小さな乗り物の乗り降りは、into と out of を用いる。
get into a car（車に乗る）、get into a taxi（タクシーに乗る）
get out of a car（車から降りる）、get out of a taxi（タクシーから降りる）
自転車の場合は、以下の表現になる。
ride (on) a bicycle（自転車に乗る）
get off a bicycle [=dismount (from) a bicycle]（自転車から降りる）

UNIT 4

Transportation

PRE-TOEIC SECTION

Vocabulary Check

次の (1) から (10) の英単語が当てはまる英文を下の (a) ～ (j) から選びなさい。

(1) abide (　　)　**(2)** accommodate (　　)　**(3)** commute (　　)
(4) consecutive (　　)　**(5)** contact (　　)　**(6)** frequent (　　)
(7) jam (　　)　**(8)** pileup (　　)　**(9)** qualification (　　)
(10) recruitment (　　)

(a) The hotel built in the center of the city can (　　) 1000 guests.
(b) The airline has a very good (　　) flyer program.
(c) We were caught in a traffic (　　) when we were in a hurry.
(d) To find good staff, companies must put a lot of effort into (　　).
(e) My child (　　)s to school by bus every day.
(f) A university degree is the minimum (　　) for this position.
(g) I had three (　　) days off, which really helped me relax.
(h) There was a (　　) of five cars at the crossroads.
(i) If something comes up, please do not hesitate to (　　) me.
(j) You must (　　) by your original purpose until it is realized.

TOEIC 語彙と語法 4　**和製英語に注意すべき場所の表現**

① ガソリンスタンド　a gas station; a filling station; a service station
② ワンルームマンション a studio apartment; a one-room apartment
③ タワーマンション a high-rise apartment building
　イギリス英語では a tower block（高層建築）とも言う。
④ スポーツクラブ　a fitness club; a gym
　I am toning up at the gym.（スポーツクラブで鍛えている）
⑤ サービスエリア、パーキングエリア　a rest area
⑥ 禁煙コーナー　a nonsmoking area　注：corner だと「隅」を意味。
⑦ ビジネスホテル　a budget hotel; a commercial hotel

LISTENING SECTION

Part 1 写真描写問題

Phase 1 Listen to the following statements and fill in the blanks.  1-41

1.

(A) Some travelers are waiting for their (   ).

(B) People are standing in five (   ).

(C) Buses are (   ) the terminal.

(D) People are all wearing (   ).

Ⓐ Ⓑ Ⓒ Ⓓ

Phase 2 1-42、43

2.

Ⓐ Ⓑ Ⓒ Ⓓ

3.

Ⓐ Ⓑ Ⓒ Ⓓ

Part 2 応答問題

Phase 1 Listen, fill in the blank and choose the best response. CD 1-44、45

4. Where can I (   ) up my car?
(A) The glass is (   ) with milk.
(B) Fill out the (   ), please.
(C) At the (   ) station over there.

5. Where did the vehicle pileup (   ) place?
(A) Paper is (   ) up on my desk.
(B) On the (   ).
(C) Any (   ) of vehicle is okay.

Phase 2 CD 1-46、47、48、49

6. Mark your answer on your answer sheet. Ⓐ Ⓑ Ⓒ

7. Mark your answer on your answer sheet. Ⓐ Ⓑ Ⓒ

8. Mark your answer on your answer sheet. Ⓐ Ⓑ Ⓒ

9. Mark your answer on your answer sheet. Ⓐ Ⓑ Ⓒ

Part 3 会話問題

Phase 1 Choose the better word that suits the blank.

(a) I took a 9:20 (flight / fright) and arrived in Tokyo at 11:30.
(b) I am planning to make a trip to Copenhagen. (How / What) do you think?
(c) I will (proceed / process) your request as soon as possible.
(d) Would it be (able / possible) for you to make an opening speech at the party?

Phase 2

10. Why will Paul take a flight?
(A) For sightseeing
(B) To meet Rosario
(C) To study abroad
(D) To attend a meeting

11. Why is Paul NOT able to take a direct flight?
(A) There are no vacant seats in business class.
(B) The airline company is on strike.
(C) There aren't any direct flights to San Francisco.
(D) The business class fare is too expensive.

12. How many frequent flyer miles does Paul have now?
(A) 515
(B) 17,000
(C) 18,000
(D) 70,000

Part 4 説明文問題

Phase 1 Fill in the blank with the most appropriate word.

(a) You can use the facility if you have a ticket (　　　　　　　) the train line.
(b) At the festival, the streets are always jammed (　　　　　　　) tourists and sightseers.
(c) Most of (　　　　　　　) smartphones in Japan are regarded as high-level devices.
(d) Some use buses that come every 30 minutes, and (　　　　　　　), taxis.

Phase 2

CD 1-52、53

13. Who most likely is the speaker?
(A) A station employee　(B) A police officer　(C) A TV director　(D) A newscaster

14. Who was most inconvenienced?
(A) Construction workers　(B) Railway passengers
(C) Taxi drivers　(D) A TV anchor

15. How was the problem overcome?
(A) Hotels offered free rooms.
(B) Everyone called their workplaces.
(C) The dump truck was soon removed.
(D) Other means of transportation were used.

Part 4 対処法②　話者と聞き手を想像する

Part 4 は会話のやりとりではなく、一方的に話しているスピーチなので、話者はどういう立場や職業の人で、語りかけている相手は、どんな人たちであるかを想像しながら、落ち着いて内容を聞くことが肝腎である。

語彙チェック 「料金」の表現

a charge 一般のサービスや労働などに対する手数料・料金
a fee 弁護士や医師など専門家のサービスに対する料金
a fare 乗り物の乗車料金、航空運賃など
a rate 単位あたりの基準によって定められた料金など
⇒ gas rates（ガス代）、water rates（水道料金）
※電気代は electric charges、水道代は water bill ということが多い。

READING SECTION

Part 5 短文穴埋問題

Phase 1 Choose the better word or phrase that suits the blank.

1. Did you enjoy (seeing / to see) the scenery from the train window?
2. I'm looking forward to (ride / riding) on the newly-refurbished cars of the express train.
3. Did you have any trouble (finding / to find) the exit of the turnpike?

Phase 2

4. My grandfather decided to quit ------- when he found his driving license expired.
(A) drive
(B) to drive
(C) driving
(D) driven

5. The drunk driver admitted not ------- by the traffic rules.
(A) abide
(B) abiding
(C) to abide
(D) abode

6. I still vividly remember ------- one month traveling with my husband across Europe.
(A) spend
(B) to spend
(C) spending
(D) spent

7. May I ------- visiting a state-of-the-art factory where AI-powered automatic vehicles are being produced?
(A) hope
(B) spend
(C) suggest
(D) insist

文法チェック **動名詞**

●重要法則・・・動名詞を目的語に取る動詞は「さける、やめる、いやがる」関連の動詞が多い

avoid doing ～（～するのを避ける）、stop doing ～（～するのをやめる）
finish doing ～（～するのを終える）、mind doing ～（～するのを気にする）
deny doing ～（～するのを否定する）、escape doing ～（～するのを逃れる）
postpone doing ～（～するのを延期する）、give up doing ～（～するのを諦める）
注：例外に enjoy doing ～（～するのを楽しむ）、appreciate doing ～（～するのを感謝する）、suggest doing ～（～するのを提案する）など。

●重要法則・・・動名詞の否定形と完了形と意味上の主語の組み合わせに注意する

a person's not having done …（人が・・・しなかったこと）

Part 6 長文穴埋問題

Phase 1 **Choose the best word that suits the blank.**

(a) The store is (existed / positioned / located) in the western part of the city.
(b) The smoke given off from the broiled meat (filled / poured / spread) the room.
(c) If you walk east for four (blocks / bricks / brooks), you will see a huge building.
(d) Nancy met an old friend of hers in the street (end / corner / margin).

Phase 2

Let me show you the way to the art museum. Exit the building -------(8.) we work. Look left for the Alfa supermarket, which is located right by where the tree-lined street begins. The sidewalks are wide enough to accommodate many shoppers. -------(9.) . Drugstores, Japanese restaurants, and fancy clothes shops -------(10.) both sides of the street, -------(11.) with tourists, especially from other Asian countries. Just walk west for four blocks. There'll be a large parking lot at the corner. From there, turn left. Then you'll find the art museum on your right. It's a large brick building.

8. (A) what
(B) where
(C) which
(D) who

9. (A) Therefore, this neighborhood is also popular with foreign tourists.
(B) Accordingly, this area is famous for being part of a marathon course.
(C) Naturally, this neighborhood doesn't have many stores.
(D) However, many people enjoy walking and shopping there.

10. (A) fix (B) fill
(C) full (D) found

11. (A) crowding
(B) crowds
(C) crawls
(D) crowded

語法チェック **前置詞の違いに注意する**

(1) at the corner of ～（～の角で、～の角に）
in the corner of ～（～の隅に） ⇒ in the corner of the room（部屋の隅に）
(2) speak to ～（～に話しかける）
speak for ～（～の代わりに話す、～を代弁する、～を弁護する）
※ be spoken for の形で「予約」の意味になる場合があるので注意。
⇒ Two seats have already been spoken for.（2 席が既に予約済みです）

Part 7 読解問題

Phase 1 Choose the best word or phrase that suits the blank.

(a) Jonathan is a former candidate (for / in / of) the position.
(b) We have (heavy / a lot / many) traffic on a few streets this morning.
(c) Our company recorded profits for three (continuing / competitive / consecutive) fiscal years.
(d) I have something to (discuss / discuss with / to be discussed) you.
(e) Don't (hesitant / hesitate / hesitation) to ask for advice.

Phase 2

Benjamin Brown

26 Bayside Road, Cardiff, UK DK77BV (030) 8755 9877email: ben.b@commonmail.com

Ms. Sophia Dahl
Metro Transportation Systems Co., Ltd.
23 Port Avenue Street
London UK

Dear Ms. Sophia Dahl,

I would like to introduce myself as a candidate for the artificial intelligence assisted sightseeing metro bus driver position at your company advertised yesterday in the London Today newspaper.

As a professional with over seven and a half years of sightseeing bus experience as well as five and a half years of professional tour guide experience, my commitment to safety and hospitality will greatly contribute to your transportation department.

For the past seven and a half years, I have been a sightseeing bus driver with West Coast Transportation Inc. and have a history of zero traffic accidents. Advanced electronic devices contributed to my accident-free driving so I am intimately familiar with such safety devices.

My comprehensive hands-on experience and historical knowledge as a professional tour guide at Pan-Pacific Travel Co., Ltd. will certainly please tourists. I also had 12 years' experience in guiding on a volunteer basis in the past. I received the in-house Best Tour Guide Award for three consecutive years. Brief examples of my skills and achievements are outlined in the attached document.

Thank you for your time and consideration. I would welcome the opportunity to discuss my qualifications in greater depth with you in the near future. Don't hesitate to contact me if you need additional information.
Sincerely,
Benjamin Brown

12. How did Benjamin Brown find the job opening?
(A) Through a recruitment agency
(B) On a website
(C) By word of mouth
(D) In a local newspaper

13. How long did Benjamin Brown work as a professional tour guide?
(A) More than seven and a half years
(B) Five years and six months
(C) Twelve years
(D) Three consecutive years

14. Which of the following qualifications or experience does Benjamin Brown NOT have?
(A) Years of teaching history on a volunteer basis
(B) A comprehensive knowledge of driving
(C) A commitment to safety and hospitality
(D) Knowledge of safety devices

語法チェック **「by ＋乗り物」で交通手段を表す**

この表現において、乗り物を表す名詞に冠詞は付かない。
by car（車で）、by taxi（タクシーで）、by bus（バスで）、by train（列車で）
by subway（地下鉄で）、by bicycle（自転車で）
注１：「徒歩で」は on foot。
注２：誰の車であるかを示す場合は in one's car を用いる。
⇒ I went for a drive in my car.（自分の車でドライブに出かけた）

UNIT 5

Post Office

PRE-TOEIC SECTION

Vocabulary Check

次の (1) から (10) の英単語が当てはまる英文を下の (a) 〜 (j) から選びなさい。

(1) available (　　)　**(2)** commemoration (　　)　**(3)** featuring (　　)
(4) handling (　　)　**(5)** inquiry (　　)　**(6)** massive (　　)
(7) respond (　　)　**(8)** treat (　　)　**(9)** upgrade (　　)
(10) weigh (　　)

(a) Would you please allow me to (　　) you to dinner next month?
(b) The planning manager took time to (　　) one plan against the other.
(c) Lunch boxes are (　　) at some stations and on some trains.
(d) Changing jobs was a good opportunity to (　　) your career.
(e) The weekly magazine (　　) the scandal sold very well.
(f) We will be holding a party in (　　) of the 20th anniversary of the foundation.
(g) It is important for us to be ready to (　　) to an emergency all the time.
(h) The president executed (　　) layoffs of 1,200 employees.
(i) The manager is good at (　　) a wide variety of jobs efficiently.
(j) Thank you for your (　　) of April 24 concerning our products.

TOEIC 語彙と語法 5　**「A を B とみなす」の表現**

① consider A to be B（A を B であるとみなす、考える）
② think A to be B（A を B であるとみなす、考える、思う）[=think of A as B]
　注：①と②において to be は B が形容詞や不定名詞句なら省略可能。
　　⇒ I consider him intellectual.（彼を知的な人とみなす）
　　　[=I consider him an intellectual man.]
③ look on A as B（A を B であるとみなす、見る）
④ regard A as B（A を B であるとみなす）
　注：as 以下に名詞句のみならず、形容詞も可能。
　　⇒ She regards Jack as smart.（彼女はジャックが賢いとみなす）

LISTENING SECTION

Part 1 写真描写問題

Phase 1 Listen to the following statements and fill in the blanks.  1-54

1.

Ⓐ Ⓑ Ⓒ Ⓓ

(A) Something is ( ) put into an envelope.

(B) A document is being ( ) out of the bag.

(C) The envelope has already been ( ).

(D) The postcard is going to be ( ).

Phase 2 1-55、56

2.

Ⓐ Ⓑ Ⓒ Ⓓ

3.

Ⓐ Ⓑ Ⓒ Ⓓ

Part 2 応答問題

Phase 1 Listen, fill in the blank and choose the best response. CD 1-57、58

4. When did you (   ) Christmas cards?
   (A) Christmas is drawing (   )
   (B) Three days (   ) Christmas Eve.
   (C) To friends who live (   ).

5. When are we supposed to receive New Year's (   ) cards?
   (A) On New Year's (   ).
   (B) Before New Year's (   ) last year.
   (C) The message reads "(   ) New Year!"

Phase 2 CD 1-59、60、61、62

6. Mark your answer on your answer sheet. Ⓐ Ⓑ Ⓒ

7. Mark your answer on your answer sheet. Ⓐ Ⓑ Ⓒ

8. Mark your answer on your answer sheet. Ⓐ Ⓑ Ⓒ

9. Mark your answer on your answer sheet. Ⓐ Ⓑ Ⓒ

Part 3 会話問題

Phase 1 Choose the better word or phrase that suits the blank.

(a) I was not (known / informed) of the fact that the meeting was cancelled.
(b) We will (handle / handle with) the problem in question among ourselves.
(c) She tried to (remind / remain) calm when the fire alarm sounded.
(d) The virus infected my files and (caused / occurred) my computer to become useless.

Phase 2

10. How many times has Veronica's computer been infected?
(A) Once
(B) Twice
(C) Four times
(D) Never

11. Which department does the woman most likely work in?
(A) Accounting
(B) Postal affairs
(C) IT
(D) Sales

12. What does the man offer to do?
(A) Fix Veronica's computer
(B) Develop new calculation apps
(C) Help Veronica calculate sales data
(D) Treat the woman to dinner

Part 4 説明文問題

Phase 1 Fill in the blank with the most appropriate word.

(a) The ceremony was conducted (　　　　　　　) commemoration of the 100th anniversary.
(b) She said that Bob was a doctor, (　　　　　　　) was found to be a complete lie.
(c) Our conversations often lead (　　　　　　　) misunderstandings.
(d) The trade fair will be held (　　　　　　　) November 23 to December 3.

Phase 2

13. Who most likely are the listeners?
(A) Curators　(B) Art lovers
(C) Stamp collectors　(D) Sculptors

14. Look at the graphic. In which room will the listeners get a stamp?
(A) Room 1　(B) Room 2
(C) Room 3　(D) Room 4

15. When will the exhibition be held?
(A) Spring　(B) Summer
(C) Fall　(D) Winter

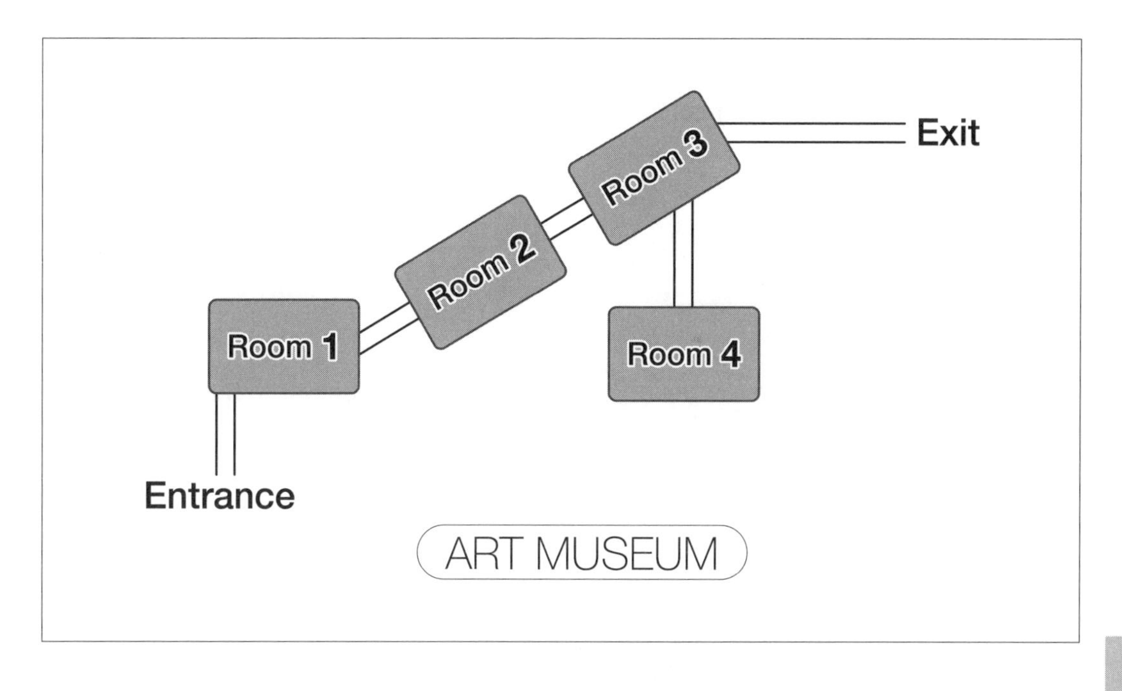

READING SECTION

Part 5 短文穴埋問題

Phase 1 Choose the better word or phrase that suits the blank.

1. You are required (to / for) pay an extra fee if you designate a delivery date.
2. On your way to school, be sure (to drop / dropping) this letter into a mailbox.
3. Remember (to weigh / weighing) a parcel before sending it.

Phase 2

4. The Ministry of Post and Telecommunications is planning ------- the postage rate for letters and postcards.
   (A) raise
   (B) raising
   (C) to raise
   (D) to raising

5. You are ------- to use registered mail if you want to send valuables.
   (A) need
   (B) supposed
   (C) considered
   (D) necessary

6. Check thoroughly if your mail includes items that are not permitted ------- overseas.
   (A) to send
   (B) sent
   (C) to be sent
   (D) sending

7. Do you intend ------- to a post office clerk about the undelivered mail?
   (A) complain
   (B) complaining
   (C) complained
   (D) to complain

語法チェック 「必要性」に関する表現

S が～する必要がある⇒ It is necessary for S to do~. (= S needs to do~.)
S が～する必要はない⇒ There is no need for S to do~.

文法チェック 不定詞

●重要法則・・・不定詞を取る動詞は願望・意志・計画など「未来を指向する」動詞が多い
desire to do ～（～することを望む）、hope to do ～（～することを希望する）
demand to do ～（～するのを要求する）、endeavor to do ～（～する努力をする）
expect to do ～（～することを期待する）、plan to do ～（～することを計画する）
remember to do ～（忘れずに～する）、forget to do ～（～するのを忘れる）
注：remember doing ～は「～したことを覚えている」、forget doing ～は「～したことを忘れている」の意味となる。

●重要法則・・・不定詞の否定形と完了形と意味上の主語の組み合わせに注意する for a person not to have done …（人が・・・しなかったこと）

Part 6 長文穴埋問題

Phase 1 Choose the best word that suits the blank.

(a) In 1957 the 100-yen silver coin was first (caste / issued / published).
(b) Mary collected various (recordable / memorial / commemorative) stamps.
(c) This year (forms / marks / signs) our 20th wedding anniversary.
(d) The person possessing the jewels met with a (flow / series / row) of misfortunes.

Phase 2

Japan's postal system was founded in 1871. The first stamps were issued in April 1871, in a set of four covering the different postal rates. The yen stamps were soon replaced by a new set of four designs -------(8.) the imperial crest. -------(9.) . Moreover, a chrysanthemum was on every Japanese stamp until 1947, -------(10.) the visage of the emperor depicted on each stamp. The first commemorative stamp, in 1894, marked the 25th anniversary of the wedding of Emperor Meiji and Empress Shoken. The first New Year's stamp in 1935 depicted Mount Fuji, -------(11.) did the first of a long-running series of national parks, appearing in 1936.

8. (A) features
(B) featuring
(C) featured
(D) feature

9. (A) Many people were happy that the imperial crest was not employed.
(B) The commemorative stamp was also issued with Mt. Fuji depicted on it.
(C) Pictures of national parks played a major role in the design of the stamps.
(D) The new designs also included Latin script for the denominations.

10. (A) due (B) in spite of
(C) instead (D) in lieu of

11. (A) unlike (B) such
(C) as (D) so

語彙チェック **郵便の表現**

速達郵便 express mail　書留郵便 registered mail
外国郵便 foreign mail　国内郵便 domestic mail
郵便為替 a (postal) money order
⇒郵便為替で X (金額) 送る：send X by money order = send a money order for X
郵便貯金 postal savings (= post-office savings)

Part 7 読解問題

Phase 1 Choose the best word that suits the blank.

(a) It will (need / require / take) me two hours to retrieve the data.

(b) The Post Office has announced that (parcel / partial / pertinent) charges will go up from this April.

(c) (Inflation / Infrastructure / Inflammable) means the basic physical and organizational facilities.

(d) He has no (tolerance / tolerate / tolerated) for mistakes.

(e) I'm keeping my fingers (cross / crossing / crossed) for your success.

Phase 2

- **Emma Abbott** ▶10:49

The post office says that outgoing parcels to Zimbabwe will arrive late because of the damage due to the serious cyclone.

- **Emma Abbott** ▶10:50

It will take two weeks longer than usual.

- **Noah Flint** ▶10:52

Oh, will express delivery make a difference?

- **Emma Abbott** ▶11:01

No, the infrastructure there is in chaos.

- **Noah Flint** ▶11:07

I expected it would take only a week as usual. Are there any other ways to get the package sent? The document absolutely must be delivered on time. The client won't tolerate delays.

- **Emma Abbott** ▶11:29

Why don't we deliver it to Mozambique first and then use an express motorbike courier service to Zimbabwe? The client lives near the border between the two countries. The post service in Mozambique seems fine.

• **Noah Flint** ▶11:35
I've just got permission from the boss. Let's give it a shot.

• **Emma Abbott** ▶11:37
Got it. I'll keep my fingers crossed.

12. What is being discussed?
(A) An important contract
(B) A document written by the client
(C) Risks of a border conflict
(D) Mail service

13. How long did Noah Flint think it would usually take to send something to Zimbabwe?
(A) About a week
(B) About two weeks
(C) About three weeks
(D) More than four weeks

14. At 11:35, what does Noah Flint mean when he writes, "Let's give it a shot"?
(A) He has decided to accept Emma's suggestion.
(B) He will fly to Zimbabwe.
(C) He will give up sending the document.
(D) He has decided to send it by express mail.

Part 7　**対処法 ②　設問先読みが大切**

設問が書かれていない Part 1 や Part 2 は設問先読みは不可能であるが、その他の Part のうち、設問先読みが効果的なのは、Part 3、Part 4、Part 6 そして Part 7 である。

特に、Part 7 はパッセージが長かったり、複数ある場合（2つ、または、3つのパッセージ）が存在するので、設問は先に読み、何が問われているかをしっかりと前もって知っておくことが大切である。

その設問の答えを探すつもりで、パッセージを読むことが重要である。

語法チェック　**time を用いた重要表現**

(1) on time 時間ぴったりに
in time 時間内に、間に合って　cf. in time for ～（～に間に合って）
(2) at a time 一度に　cf. at times（時々）
at one time かつて、昔（は）

UNIT 6

Bank

PRE-TOEIC SECTION

Vocabulary Check

次の (1) から (10) の英単語が当てはまる英文を下の (a) ～ (j) から選びなさい。

(1) depiction (　　)
(2) discontinue (　　)
(3) deposit (　　)
(4) integration (　　)
(5) merge (　　)
(6) popularity (　　)
(7) range (　　)
(8) remittance (　　)
(9) teller (　　)
(10) withdraw (　　)

(a) The blue whale (　　)s from 20 to 30 meters in length.
(b) It is a real pity to (　　) a job that has made so much progress.
(c) The American ten dollar bill has a (　　) of Alexander Hamilton on it.
(d) She was not able to (　　) money from her ordinary bank account.
(e) Getting the answer we need will require the (　　) of three sets of data.
(f) She asked the (　　) about the interest rate on the short term loan.
(g) Online games of Japanese chess have recently gained in (　　).
(h) He converted a part of the money in his ordinary account into a fixed-term (　　).
(i) We believe that you will receive the (　　) the day after tomorrow.
(j) A vote was held to decide whether the village should (　　) with the town.

TOEIC 語彙と語法 6　会社内の役職の英語

① 平社員 an ordinary employee; a rank and file member of staff
② 主任　a chief; a head
③ 課長　a section chief
④ 課長代理　an acting head of the section
⑤ 部長　a manager
⑥ 部長代理　an acting manager
⑦ 専務、常務　a managing director
⑧ 副社長　a vice-president
⑨ 社長、最高経営責任者　president; CEO (Chief Executive Officer)

LISTENING SECTION

Part 1 写真描写問題

Phase 1 Listen to the following statements and fill in the blanks.  1-67

1.

Ⓐ Ⓑ Ⓒ Ⓓ

(A) There's someone ( ) currency.

(B) The bank is ( ).

(C) A lot of people are ( ) in front of the bank.

(D) Some people are window ( ).

Phase 2  1-68、69

2.

Ⓐ Ⓑ Ⓒ Ⓓ

3.

Ⓐ Ⓑ Ⓒ Ⓓ

Part 2 応答問題

Phase 1 Listen, fill in the blank and choose the best response. CD 1-70、71

4. Why are there so many people in (　　　　　　) at the ATM?
　(A) The supermarket was very (　　　　　　).
　(B) To (　　　　　　) money.
　(C) Because the ATM was out of (　　　　　　).

5. Why couldn't you open an (　　　　　　) at the bank?
　(A) Because I forgot to bring my (　　　　　　).
　(B) (　　　　　　) it to my account.
　(C) All companies have to (　　　　　　) accountability.

Phase 2 CD 1-72、73、74、75

6. Mark your answer on your answer sheet. Ⓐ Ⓑ Ⓒ

7. Mark your answer on your answer sheet. Ⓐ Ⓑ Ⓒ

8. Mark your answer on your answer sheet. Ⓐ Ⓑ Ⓒ

9. Mark your answer on your answer sheet. Ⓐ Ⓑ Ⓒ

Part 3 会話問題

Phase 1 Choose the better word that suits the blank.

(a) I (transmitted / transferred) 100,000 yen to my landlord's bank account.
(b) Would you tell me the address and name of the (branch / brunch) to be paid?
(c) Surprisingly, the bank charge was a lot higher (at / with) 760 yen.
(d) The expenses and fees of the patent attorney were (lawyer / lower) than I expected.

Phase 2

10. What is most likely the relationship between the man and the woman?
(A) Customer and bank teller
(B) Banker and investor
(C) Loan officer and applicant
(D) Colleagues at the same bank

11. Where does the man want to transfer money?
(A) To his bank account
(B) To a branch of Marubishi Bank
(C) To a branch of Stardust Bank
(D) To Hirakata Bank

12. How much will the man have to pay for the service?
(A) 540 yen
(B) 750 yen
(C) 860 yen
(D) 369,000 yen

Part 4 説明文問題

Phase 1 Fill in the blank with the most appropriate word.

(a) Working in cooperation (　　　　　　) his friend Jack, John was able to finish the report before the deadline.
(b) (　　　　　　) who buy this product are entitled to get a 10-percent discount.
(c) The area is characterized by high-grade amenities such (　　　　　　) cinemas and museums.
(d) The computer here is available for use (　　　　　　) a whole day.

Phase 2

13. What kind of service does the speaker provide?
(A) Credit card
(B) Eco-friendly facial tissues
(C) Towel disposal
(D) Term deposits

14. What is the period of time in which the customer can purchase the service?
(A) Five years
(B) Four months
(C) Three days
(D) The month of August

15. What limited item can customers get?
(A) An eco-friendly product
(B) A towel with an athlete's likeness
(C) A teddy bear mascot doll
(D) An electronic device

語法チェック 「A は B を特徴とする」の表現

A is featured by B. (= B features A)
A is characterized by B (=B characterizes A)
B is characteristic of A

READING SECTION

Part 5 短文穴埋問題

Phase 1 Choose the better word that suits the blank.

1. I can (hard / hardly) wait for the opening of the new branch of the bank.
2. (Fortunate / Fortunately), the time deposit I had with the bank increased at a compound interest rate.
3. Ever (since / from) Quartz Bank closed, I have never heard of any bank going bankrupt.

Phase 2

4. Salaries for all employees are transferred ------- into their bank accounts.
   (A) direct (B) directing
   (C) directly (D) direction

5. The bank is planning to ------- release an array of new financial services.
   (A) currently (B) previously
   (C) officially (D) probably

6. Ms. Whitman ------- asked the teller to give her the rate of interest on a fixed-term deposit.
   (A) hurry (B) hurries
   (C) hurried (D) hurriedly

7. The bank announced that ------- March 31, the senior managing director would step down to take responsibility for the bribery scandal.
   (A) effect (B) effective
   (C) effectiveness (D) effectively

Part 5 対処法 ② どんな品詞が空所に入るのかを常に考える

冠詞と形容詞の間に空所があれば副詞 (very や…ly 型)、冠詞と名詞の間に空所があれば形容詞、文頭に空所があり、選択肢が 1 語であれば、通常、文副詞が来るので、ly 型の単語を選ぶとよいことになる。

文法チェック **副詞**

●重要法則・・・助動詞や不定詞の to の直後、一般動詞の直前につく副詞が多い
can hardly understand ～（～が殆ど分からない）[hardly は程度の低さを表す]
seldom eat vegetables（野菜を殆ど食べない）[seldom は頻度の低さを表す]
hope to fully understand ～（～を十分に理解したい）

●重要法則・・・文頭に現れる副詞は、話者の気持ちを表す場合が多い
Happily, John didn't die.（幸せにも、ジョンは死ななかった）
[happily は文副詞で文全体を修飾]
John didn't die happily.（ジョンは幸せには死ななかった）
[happily は die を修飾する様態副詞⇒「ジョンは不幸な死に方をした」の意]

Part 6 長文穴埋問題

Phase 1 Choose the best word that suits the blank.

(a) I (dismissed / disposed / discontinued) my subscription to the newspaper.
(b) The (unified / monism / oneness) systems made our business successful.
(c) We have to make some (flight / plight / slight) changes to better the situation.
(d) An illustrated catalog was (disclosed / enclosed / reclosed) in the envelope.

Phase 2

To all our customers:

Thank you very much for using our service.

Since we -------- (8.) with Owl Bank last October, we have been offering two separate online banking services, our own proprietary model and that of Owl Bank's. However, we have decided to discontinue both of these and create a new unified service as of Feb. 10. -------- (9.) .

During the preparation for the integration of services, there may -------- (10.) temporary cessations of other online services. Also, there will be some slight changes made to these other services which may require you to follow new guidelines. All information regarding -------- (11.) that apply to upcoming changes is available in the leaflet enclosed in this letter.

We must apologize to all of you for this inconvenience. Simultaneously, we look forward to offering you a more efficient and hassle-free banking experience in the future.

8. (A) dealt (B) coped
(C) bonded (D) merged

9. (A) The older services will continue to be available for new customers.
(B) This is to offer the same high quality service in all our branches.
(C) That's why we became independent of Owl Bank on Feb. 10.
(D) That's because system integration is not really necessary.

10. (A) occur (B) cause
(C) well (D) not

11. (A) some (B) them
(C) ones (D) those

Part 7 読解問題

Phase 1 Choose the best word or phrase that suits the blank.

(a) Artificial intelligence will eliminate bank (talker / teller / taller) jobs.
(b) The number of cash transactions (is / are / has) decreasing.
(c) I am worried about whether I can finish it by the (dew / do / due date).
(d) My supervisor (lend / lent / rented) that condo for $2,000 a month.
(e) The new product has been introduced (in / on / within) time for the Christmas shopping season.

Phase 2

• **Liam Chung** ▶10:11
Hi, I'm at the East Coast Bank. I'm afraid I can't send money to you today. The bank's computers have been experiencing system errors all day.

• **Olivia Emerson** ▶10:15
I see. Will they be open tomorrow?

• **Liam Chung** ▶10:17
Yes. A bank teller says I can apply for a remittance today but the transaction itself will be processed tomorrow.

• **Olivia Emerson** ▶10:19
That'd be great. Please make sure to keep the due date in mind.

• **Liam Chung** ▶10:20
Sure thing. I'll be on time next month, though this month will be a little late.

• **Olivia Emerson** ▶10:22
I see. By the way, how's the air conditioner that was installed last month?

• **Liam Chung** ▶10:23
Can't complain.

• **Olivia Emerson** ▶10:25
OK. Enjoy your stay in Chicago.

12. What prevented Liam Chung from remitting money?
(A) A bank teller's mistake
(B) A national holiday
(C) System failure
(D) A due date change

13. What is most likely Olivia Emerson's job?
(A) A landlady
(B) A lessee
(C) A moneylender
(D) A bank teller

14. At 10:23 A.M., what does Liam Chung mean when he writes, "Can't complain"?
(A) The air conditioner works properly.
(B) The air conditioner doesn't work well.
(C) He wants to complain about it.
(D) He wants to complain but he can't.

Part 7 対処法 ③ SNS問題は口語的表現が出るので注意

本文では、Can't complain が出ているが、普段から口語表現に着目しておくことが大切である。しかし、かなり砕けた俗語やマイナスイメージの言葉は出題されない。

語彙チェック 多義語の bill と note に着目

(1) bill 紙幣、勘定書き、請求書、ビラ、広告、（演劇などの）プログラム
為替手形 (bill of exchange) [=draft]
(2) note 紙幣、覚え書き、記録、メモ、（正式な）文書、通達、（本文の）注
約束手形（promissory note）

UNIT 7

Airport

PRE-TOEIC SECTION

Vocabulary Check

次の (1) から (10) の英単語が当てはまる英文を下の (a) ～ (j) から選びなさい。

(1) await (　　)　**(2)** complimentary (　　)　**(3)** consist (　　)
(4) deserve (　　)　**(5)** efficient (　　)　**(6)** entitle (　　)
(7) laptop (　　)　**(8)** quarter (　　)　**(9)** receptionist (　　)
(10) runway (　　)

(a) I (　　) your response on the matter I talked about yesterday.
(b) Whenever I travel abroad, I take my (　　) with me.
(c) The advisory committee (　　)-s of ten members.
(d) The airplane in trouble safely touched down on the (　　).
(e) The store distributed (　　) shopping tickets to its stockholders.
(f) The (　　) told me to sign my name on the paper.
(g) The honor you are giving me is more than I (　　).
(h) Business dropped off drastically in the second (　　).
(i) Products that are highly energy-(　　) are now a focus of public attention.
(j) Sally's outstanding work record (　　)-s her to the respect of all her colleagues.

TOEIC 語彙と語法 7　会社内の部署の英語

① 営業部、販売部　the sales department
② 人事部　the HR department [=the human resources department];
　the personnel department
③ 経理部　the accounting department
④ 企画部　the planning department
⑤ マーケッティング部　the marketing department
⑥ 研究開発部　the R & D department [=the research and development department]
⑦ 総務部　the general affairs department
※「部」を「課」とする場合は、department を section とする。

LISTENING SECTION

Part 1 写真描写問題

Phase 1 Listen to the following statements and fill in the blanks.

1-80

1.

Ⓐ Ⓑ Ⓒ Ⓓ

(A) The plane is taking ( ) from the airport.

(B) The sky is perfectly ( ).

(C) Some ( ) are in front of the plane.

(D) Passengers are now ( ).

Phase 2 1-81､82

2.

Ⓐ Ⓑ Ⓒ Ⓓ

3.

Ⓐ Ⓑ Ⓒ Ⓓ

Part 2 応答問題

Phase 1 Listen, fill in the blank and choose the best response. CD 1-83、84

4. How are business (   ) flights?
   (A) Business hotels are (   ) expensive.
   (B) Very (   ).
   (C) Business as (   ).

5. How can I (   ) to the airport from here?
   (A) By (   ) bus or taxi.
   (B) Yes, you can get there (   ) 20 minutes.
   (C) Present a (   ) pass.

Phase 2 CD 1-85、86、87、88

6. Mark your answer on your answer sheet. Ⓐ Ⓑ Ⓒ
7. Mark your answer on your answer sheet. Ⓐ Ⓑ Ⓒ
8. Mark your answer on your answer sheet. Ⓐ Ⓑ Ⓒ
9. Mark your answer on your answer sheet. Ⓐ Ⓑ Ⓒ

Part 3 会話問題

Phase 1 Choose the better word that suits the blank.

(a) She had no (chance / choice) but to agree, though she didn't want to.
(b) The Japanese population began to (decline / weaken) in 2005.
(c) The membership of the association is (in / on) the increase.
(d) I want to (put / turn) up some good numbers in sales this year.

Phase 2

10. Why did Rosa and Shane give up on their trip to Hawaii?
(A) They became ill.
(B) They couldn't change their days off.
(C) They failed to book a flight.
(D) Shane's work interrupted their plans.

11. Look at the graphic. During which quarter did sales start to decline?
(A) The first
(B) The second
(C) The third
(D) The fourth

12. What will the speakers probably do next?
(A) Go on a business trip
(B) Call a travel agent
(C) Reschedule the sales conference
(D) Give a bonus to their staff

Meeting Plans

First Quarter	Winter • Planning meeting
Second Quarter	Spring • Sales Meeting I
Third Quarter	Summer • Sales Meeting 2
Fourth Quarter	Autumn • Sales Conference

Part 4 説明文問題

Phase 1 Fill in the blank with the most appropriate word.

(a) I sincerely apologize to you (　　　　　　) having made a serious mistake.
(b) The product made of iron is now covered (　　　　　　) rust.
(c) Please (　　　　　　) free to ask any question regarding my explanation.
(d) I have to get a lot of work done (　　　　　　) my computer by tomorrow.

Phase 2

13. Who most likely are the listeners?
(A) Cabin crew
(B) Guests
(C) Shoppers
(D) Passengers

14. What is the condition of the runway?
(A) It is flooded.
(B) The weather caused it to freeze.
(C) It is impeded by snow.
(D) Birds have intruded onto it.

15. What service can business-class passengers take advantage of?
(A) Duty-free goods offered at a discount
(B) Drinks on the house
(C) A free round-trip ticket
(D) A free stay at the airport hotel

READING SECTION

Part 5 短文穴埋問題

Phase 1 Choose the best word or phrase that fits in the blank.

1. I bought brand-name cosmetics at the shop, which was (crowded / crowding) with tourists.
2. The airfare was disappointingly higher than (expecting / expected).
3. Having (complete / completed) the check-in process, I went to the business-class lounge.

Phase 2

4. Here are the immigration procedures ------- of all visitors to this country.
   (A) require
   (B) requirement
   (C) required
   (D) requiring

5. I got an e-mail ------- that the flight I had requested was booked to capacity.
   (A) say (B) said
   (C) saying (D) to say

6. Deeply ------- at the lack of privileges available for frequent fliers, I have decided to leave the club.
   (A) disappoint
   (B) disappointed
   (C) disappointing
   (D) disappointment

7. The typhoon was approaching the Japanese archipelago, ------- all flights to and from the airport.
   (A) cancel
   (B) cancellation
   (C) cancelled
   (D) cancelling

文法チェック **分詞**

●重要法則・・・文の構造に直接関わる場合と修飾（形容詞的と副詞的）をするものに分類でき、文の構造は以下のものを作る

be ＋現在分詞 (doing …) ⇒ 進行形（～している）

be ＋過去分詞 (done …) ⇒ 受動態（～される）

have ＋過去分詞 (done …) ⇒ 完了形（完了・経験・継続の意味）

●重要法則・・・名詞句に関わる場合（形容詞的修飾）、分詞１語は前から、分詞が導く句は後から名詞句を修飾する

the sleeping baby（その眠っている赤ん坊）

the baby sleeping in bed（ベッドで寝ている赤ん坊）

注：a sleeping car（寝台車）における sleeping は現在分詞ではなく、動名詞。だから、a sleeping car を a car for sleeping と言い換えることができる。

●重要法則・・・副詞的修飾をする場合は分詞構文と呼ばれるが、分詞構文の否定形と完了形と意味上の主語を表した形に特に注意する

a person not having done …（ある人が…をしなかったので / しなかったとき）

Part 6 長文穴埋問題

Phase 1 Choose the best word or phrase that suits the blank.

(a) I went to the shop directly after going through (custom / a custom / customs).

(b) You can see a number of high-rise condominiums (at / on / in) the right.

(c) A variety of (stills / stalls / strolls) are set up during the festival.

(d) You can relax in a gorgeous (ranch / lounge / launch) on the top floor.

Phase 2

I'll explain about how our airport handles new arrivals. After going through customs, passengers turn left and --8.-- an escalator down to the first floor. --9.-- . After picking up their suitcases, passengers exit the lobby to the terminal. On the right, they will find restaurants and souvenir shops. On the second floor, there are also various Japanese restaurants and Western-style cafes near the waiting area, --10.-- takoyaki and okonomiyaki stalls for those that like Osaka cuisine. Going up to the third floor, passengers can relax while receiving a massage or manicure. Also there, a luxurious business lounge awaits business travelers for --11.-- .

8. (A) put　　(B) reach
(C) take　　(D) have

9. (A) You can see a ticket counter in the back.
(B) An elevator in front of you will take you back up.
(C) Relax at the business lounge in front of you.
(D) There is a baggage carousel directly in front.

10. (A) containing
(B) including
(C) consisting
(D) holding

11. (A) freedom　　(B) freely
(C) freed　　(D) free

語法チェック　**reach の語法**

(a) 他動詞としての用法 ･･･ 前置詞は用いない
reach ～ ～に到着する [=get to ～ /arrive at ～]、結論などに達する、数量が～に及ぶ
⇒ The total number reached 2 million.（総数が 2 百万に及んだ）
(b) 自動詞としての用法 ･･･ 副詞句を用いる
reach (out) for ～ ～を取ろうと手を伸ばす / reach after fame 名声を求める

Part 7 読解問題

Phase 1 Choose the best word that suits the blank.

(a) May I see your (board / boarding / boating) pass, please?
(b) My boss regards subordinates (as / for / of) servants.
(c) It sounds strange but these two theories are mutually (exclude / excluding / exclusive).
(d) Soft drinks are (complimentary / complete / compliance) , so no payment is required.
(e) Our current procedures are far from (efficient / efficiently / efficiency).

Phase 2

e-mail

To: Jack Adams <j.adams@freemail.com>
From: Jackson Allen <j.allen@bananaairline.com>
Date: September 7
Subject: Upgrade membership notification

Dear Mr. Jack Adams,
Thank you for your frequent patronage of Banana Airlines. We are pleased to announce that your membership has been upgraded to Platinum status, giving you access to 157 lounges worldwide. You will find a Platinum Member lounge with state-of-the-art electronic devices at most major airports.
We regard our loyal customers' privacy and time as vitally important. Each lounge is exclusive to Platinum Members and has spacious private rooms, each of which is enclosed by soundproof walls.
Let us briefly introduce our other facilities, food and drinks, and available services.
-Shower suites and saunas
-High-speed secure internet connection
-Computers with 4K monitors
-Complimentary beverages
-A variety of meal and snack options
-Concierge
-Massage

On top of this is a service that deserves a special mention. We have introduced a round-the-clock catering service. Japanese, French, Spanish, and Mexican cuisine are available anytime for you to enjoy at a private lounge.
We have tentatively introduced an AI concierge. It will answer your questions or requests via vocal input. All facilities, such as massage chairs, lights, music, TV, and the air conditioner in your private room will be controlled by your voice.
Last but not least, facial recognition authentication has been introduced. Please register your face on your first visit to the lounge in order to enjoy our platinum services. Please ask our receptionists about face registration in order to begin.
We hope you will enjoy an exclusive lounge experience and use your valuable time efficiently. We will make every effort to make your trip more comfortable.

Sincerely Yours,
Jackson Allen
CEO, Banana Airlines

12. What is the main purpose of this e-mail?
(A) To ask Jack Adams to pay an annual membership fee
(B) To give notification of a change in membership status
(C) To introduce new facilities and services
(D) To upgrade facilities in lounges

13. In the e-mail, the word "state-of-the-art" in paragraph 1, line 4, is closest in meaning to
(A) expensive
(B) gorgeous
(C) latest
(D) artistic

14. What is NOT included to the platinum membership services and facilities?
(A) free drinks
(B) Electronic devices with artificial intelligence
(C) 24-hour food delivery service
(D) Fingerprint authentication

15. What should Mr. Jack Adams do first at the lounge?
(A) Talk to a receptionist
(B) Register his face
(C) Obtain a member's card
(D) Ask the AI concierge any questions

UNIT 8

Hotel

PRE-TOEIC SECTION

Vocabulary Check

次の (1) から (10) の英単語が当てはまる英文を下の (a) ～ (j) から選びなさい。

(1) affiliate (　　)　**(2)** amenities (　　)　**(3)** banquet (　　)
(4) brochure (　　)　**(5)** buffet (　　)　**(6)** compatible (　　)
(7) concierge (　　)　**(8)** fair (　　)　**(9)** line (　　)
(10) suite (　　)

(a) I would appreciate it if you could send me a (　　) and price information.
(b) This software is not (　　) with our newly developed system.
(c) I will invite you to this trade (　　) as you can learn a lot about the products.
(d) With its wide range of (　　), the hotel is popular among businesspersons.
(e) A hotel (　　) helps guests get everything they need during their stay.
(f) Tom was so rich that he reserved the hotel (　　) for himself for ten nights.
(g) The large Japanese-style room in this restaurant functions as a (　　) room.
(h) We held a simple (　　)-style dinner, which made all our customers happy.
(i) I am grateful to the customers and all (　　) parties for your patronage.
(j) All the books that she bought are (　　)d up on this book shelf.

TOEIC 語彙と語法 8　**数えられない名詞（不可算で複数形なし）**

① 基本的な形がないので数えられない名詞（物質名詞と抽象名詞）
water（水）、wood（木）、beef（牛肉）、advice（助言）、fun（楽しさ）
② 小さく分解しても同じものと言えるので数えられない名詞
chalk（チョーク）：chalk は２つに割っても chalk（数える意味がない）
※ pencil は２つに割ったらもはや pencil とは言えない（⇒可算名詞）
③ 色々なものやことをまとめて表すので数えられない名詞
furniture（家具）、equipment（装置）、information（情報）
④ 個々の物をまとめて集合的に表すので数えられない名詞
jewelry（宝石類）[１個は a jewel]、mythology（神話）[１つは a myth]

LISTENING SECTION

Part 1 写真描写問題

Phase 1 Listen to the following statements and fill in the blanks. 

1.

Ⓐ Ⓑ Ⓒ Ⓓ

(A) There are no pillows on ( ) of the beds.

(B) There are pictures of ( ) on the walls.

(C) The two beds have ( ) been used by guests.

(D) The two flowers are in a ( ).

Phase 2 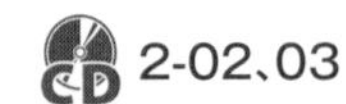

2.

Ⓐ Ⓑ Ⓒ Ⓓ

3.

Ⓐ Ⓑ Ⓒ Ⓓ

Part 2 応答問題

Phase 1 Listen, fill in the blank and choose the best response. CD 2-04、05

4. How many (　　　　　　) are you going to stay?
(A) Two (　　　　　　) days, please.
(B) (　　　　　　) only.
(C) I booked a (　　　　　　) room.

5. How late (　　　　　　) the rooftop bar open?
(A) As (　　　　　　) as ten in the morning.
(B) Until (　　　　　　), according to this brochure.
(C) The night (　　　　　　) from there is magnificent.

Phase 2 CD 2-06、07、08、09

6. Mark your answer on your answer sheet. Ⓐ Ⓑ Ⓒ

7. Mark your answer on your answer sheet. Ⓐ Ⓑ Ⓒ

8. Mark your answer on your answer sheet. Ⓐ Ⓑ Ⓒ

9. Mark your answer on your answer sheet. Ⓐ Ⓑ Ⓒ

Part 2 対処法 ② 答えかなと思ったらすぐチェック

最初の選択肢 (A) が答えかなと思ったら、鉛筆で薄くチェックし、思わなかったら、そのままにして、(B) が答えかなと思ったらチェックし、ここで答えと思わなかったら、(C) が答えである可能性が高い。どれも答えに感じなかったら、何でもよいから答えとしてマークし、気にせず、次の問題に対処する。

Part 3 会話問題

Phase 1 Choose the better word that suits the blank.

(a) I would like to reserve a (simple / single) room for two nights.
(b) He is (facing / heading) over to the meeting place.
(c) You have to pay the participation fee at the (venue / venture).
(d) Thank you for (remembering / reminding) me. I almost forgot.

Phase 2

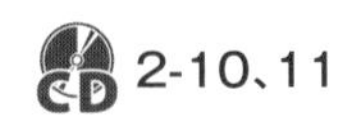

10. When is Jack going to meet Ms. Coleman?
(A) October 4th
(B) October 5th
(C) October 6th
(D) October 7th

11. What is planned on the night of October 7th?
(A) A meeting with Mr. Adams
(B) A visit to the trade fair
(C) A meeting with Ms. Coleman
(D) An inspection tour of a factory

12. What is most likely the relationship between Jack and Natasha?
(A) Salesperson and customer
(B) Manager and secretary
(C) Hotel clerk and guest
(D) Plant manager and crew

Part 4 説明文問題

Phase 1 Fill in the blank with the most appropriate word.

(a) The five-star hotel is closest (   ) the station.
(b) (   ) your left you can see a beautiful mountain called Mt. Fuji.
(c) Mr. Watt was sitting next (   ) Ms. Green at the party.
(d) On (   ) opposite side of the street was a large department store.

Phase 2

13. What is the purpose of the announcement?
(A) To explain the schedule of the sales sessions
(B) To announce guest speakers
(C) To show where a dinner party will be held
(D) To provide details of a buffet-style breakfast

14. According to the speaker, what kind of food can diners get near the speech platform?
(A) French (B) Japanese (C) Chinese (D) Italian

15. Look at the graphic. Which is the area serving Chinese dishes?
(A) Area A (B) Area B (C) Area C (D) Area D

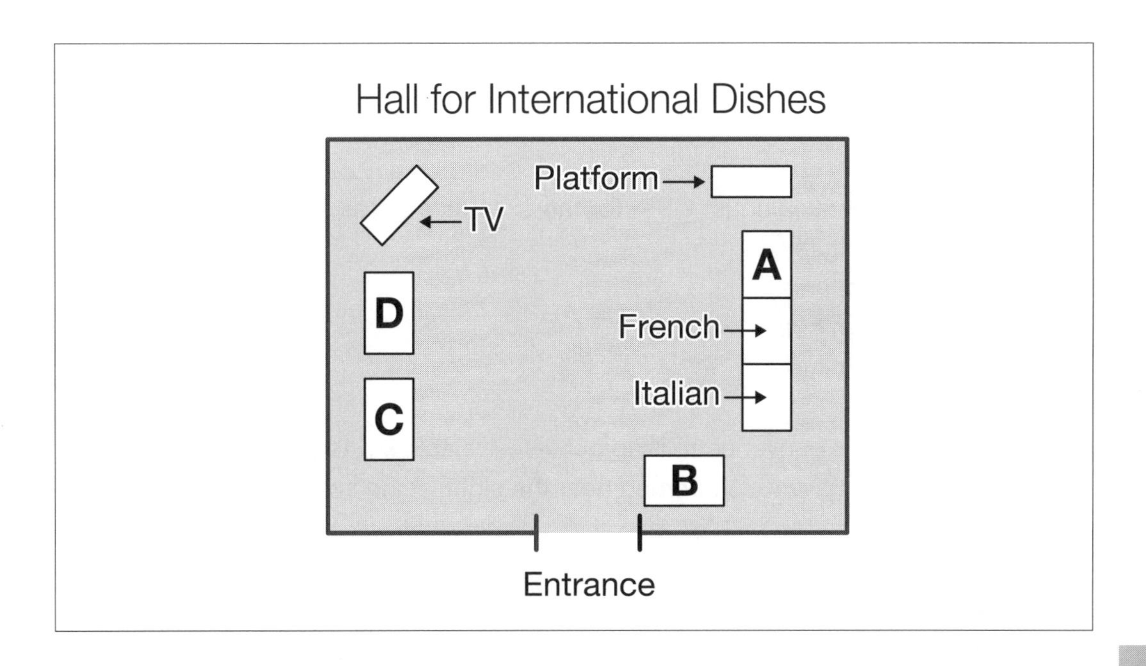

READING SECTION

Part 5 短文穴埋問題

Phase 1 Choose the better word or phrase that suits the blank.

1. I hear (thousand / thousands of) guests are staying at this hotel.
2. The store on the ground floor sells (elegant jewelry / an elegant jewelry).
3. We'll have our porters bring your (baggage / baggages) downstairs before you check out.

Phase 2

4. The good news ------- that many hotels offer a courteous service for both domestic and international guests.
(A) is
(B) are
(C) have been
(D) has

5. Concierges always stand ready at the front desk to offer good ------- to guests on various matters and various hotel facilities.
(A) advice
(B) advices
(C) advise
(D) advises

6. We need to order luxurious ------- for the executive suites on the top floor.
(A) piece of furniture
(B) piece of furnitures
(C) pieces of furniture
(D) pieces of furnitures

7. The meeting was convened to map out ------- viable strategies to cope with the new hotels that have mushroomed near the sightseeing spot.
(A) dozen
(B) some dozen
(C) dozens
(D) dozen number of

文法チェック 名詞の可算・不可算

●重要法則 ･･･ 可算名詞は、冠詞との関わりにおいては、次の４つの形を持つ。

	単　数	複　数
不定	不定冠詞＋ N：a table	無冠詞＋ N：tables
定	定冠詞＋ N：the table	定冠詞＋ N：the tables

※「定」については、the の代わりに one's や this (these) なども可能。

●重要法則 ･･･ 不可算名詞は、複数の概念がないので、「無冠詞単数形」と「定冠詞＋単数形」の２つの形しかない。

⇒ water（[不特定の] 水）、the water（[特定の] 水）

※不可算名詞は、特別の数え方をする。

⇒ a cup of tea（カップ一杯の [紅] 茶）、three pieces of furniture（家具３点）

Part 6 長文穴埋問題

Phase 1 Choose the best word that suits the blank.

(a) In Japan you need not to give a (chip / tip / zip) for good service.
(b) The toilet did not (flash / flush / flow) due to mechanical trouble.
(c) We have to be careful about the dress (cord / code / chord) at a formal party.
(d) The fashionable hotel has many (bucket / bouquet / banquet) halls.

Phase 2

Tips for Hotel Patrons

When you arrive at the hotel and the doorman opens the door, you should give him a tip. The recommended amount is about $1or $2. -------- (8.) .The items to be checked are as follows: whether the toilet flushes properly, whether the air conditioner works, and if the shower has hot water.

When -------- (9.) a restaurant, you must check the dress code. You don't have to worry if it's casual, but if the staff says, "business casual," sandals and jeans should be avoided. In the case of "business attire," jackets, slacks, and leather shoes are needed.

------- (10.) Wi-Fi is available in all guestrooms, lobbies, restaurants, and banquet halls. Parking fees are $10 per hour for restaurant customers and $15 per night for hotel ------- (11.) .

8. (A) If you should enter your room, you will have to search for amenities.
(B) When you enter your room, check the amenities.
(C) After entering the room, you should not use the amenities.
(D) Upon entering the room, ask the front desk about amenities.

9. (A) booking (B) booked (C) to book (D) having booked

10. (A) Complement (B) Compliment
(C) Complementary (D) Complimentary

11. (A) passengers (B) customers (C) guests (D) spectators

語彙チェック **一文字違いの重要語**

(a) compliment（お世辞）と complement（補完、補語）
(b) stationery（文房具）と stationary（静止した、動かない）
(c) farther（[空間的に]より遠くへ）と further（[程度が]更に進んで）
(d) fragrant（香りが良い）と flagrant（言語道断の）

Part 7 読解問題

Phase 1 Choose the best word that suits the blank.

(a) Jack owns a lot of (property / properly / proper) in Texas.
(b) I think baseball is the most (challenge / challenged / challenging) sport.
(c) Steve wrote a novel based (with / at / on) fact.
(d) The mechanic (small / fine / tiny) -tuned the engine.
(e) The company (employees / employers / employs) a new method to analyze sales figures.

Phase 2

Guest Experience Enhanced at Best Season Hotels with Mobile Access Solution

An electronic entry system enables guests to use their smartphones as room keys. —[1]—. This system is used at some of our hotels, including our franchise hotels totaling 30 properties with over 2,000 doors worldwide as of 1 January 2019.

The biggest challenge for us is to introduce an entry system compatible with the broadest possible range of smartphones as keys for guests to access their hotel rooms and our facilities, such as gyms, lounges, and storage rooms.

Our partner, AB&B Communications, has developed a mobile entry system based on major smartphone operating systems, such as iOS and Android. —[2]—. However, a bit of fine-tuning is required for other smartphone operating systems.

—[3]—. The company will create the best possible solution employing mobile device technologies that are universally accessible, easy to deploy, and easy to use for all including physically challenged people. By focusing on its technological strengths, the Best Season Hotel group is rapidly rolling out keyless entry systems to be available for 5,000 doors in 70 hotels in 2020.

—[4]—. Our keyless entry system is one of our attempts to reach this goal.

12. What is indicated as the biggest challenge?
   (A) Making a new technology compatible with more phones
   (B) Maintaining the number of hotels including affiliated branches
   (C) Finding missing room keys quickly
   (D) Enhancing the quality of hotel facilities

13. Why did Best Season Hotel partner with AB&B Communications?
   (A) AB&B Communications has an impressive history of challenging goals.
   (B) AB&B Communications developed a franchise system in the hotel industry.
   (C) AB&B Communications manufactures state-of-the-art smartphones.
   (D) AB&B Communications is familiar with mobile device technology.

14. In which of the positions marked [1], [2], [3], and [4] does the following sentence best belong? "The Best Season Hotel group is piloting innovations which empower guests to control aspects of their stay."
   (A) [1]
   (B) [2]
   (C) [3]
   (D) [4]

語法チェック **familiar と known の重要語法**

(a A is familiar with B (A は B をよく知っている)
(b) A is familiar to B (A は B によく知られている)
(c) A is known for B (A は B で知られている)
(d) A is known to B (A は B に知られている)
(e) A is known as B (A は B として知られている)
(f) A is known by B (A は B を見れば分かる)
→ A man is known by his friend.（人は友達を見れば分かる）
A tree is known by its fruit.（木はその実で分かる）

UNIT 9

Hospital

PRE-TOEIC SECTION

Vocabulary Check

次の (1) から (10) の英単語が当てはまる英文を下の (a) ～ (j) から選びなさい。

(1) checkup (　　)　(2) classified (　　)　(3) diagnose (　　)
(4) hospitalize (　　)　(5) indispensable (　　)　(6) instrument (　　)
(7) memorize (　　)　(8) prescribe (　　)　(9) replace (　　)
(10) surgery (　　)

(a) The technical terms in the field of medicine are difficult to (　　).
(b) My father is going to have a specific medical (　　) next month.
(c) The (　　) was performed on her second admission to the clinic.
(d) X-rays are often used to help medical doctors (　　) disease.
(e) Japanese gardens can be roughly (　　) into three groups.
(f) He (　　)d painkillers for the patient suffering from a severe headache.
(g) Basic information about Japanese religions is (　　) to tourist guides in Japan.
(h) This is a tube used as a medical (　　) and is inserted into the stomach.
(i) The time may come when doctors and pharmacists are (　　)d by AI.
(j) The acting manager was (　　)d for diagnosis and treatment.

TOEIC 語彙と語法 9　意味が似ている重要単語

① tool（道具）、implement（用具）、instrument（器具）[この順に精巧になる]
　⇒ writing implement（筆記用具）、medical instrument（医療器具）
② study（[個々の] 研究）、research（[全体的な] 研究）
　⇒ research（通例不可算）は a study の集合体と言える。
③ rest（疲れたから取る休憩）、break（疲れていなくても取る休憩）
　⇒ You look tired. Let's take a rest.（仕事の合間の休憩とは限らない）
④ 有名な：well-known、famous、renowned の順にプラスイメージ
　⇒ infamous は「有名でない」ではなく「悪評高い」。
⑤ valueless は「無価値の」、invaluable は「非常に価値が高い」

LISTENING SECTION

Part 1 写真描写問題

Phase 1 Listen to the following statements and fill in the blanks. 

1.

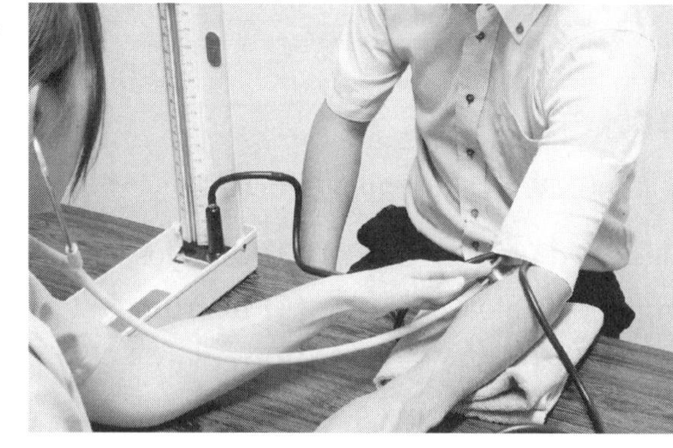

Ⓐ Ⓑ Ⓒ Ⓓ

(A) The device needs to be ( ) in.

(B) Two people are ( ) up.

(C) Blood pressure is being ( ).

(D) The nurse is taking her ( ).

Phase 2 2-15、16

2.

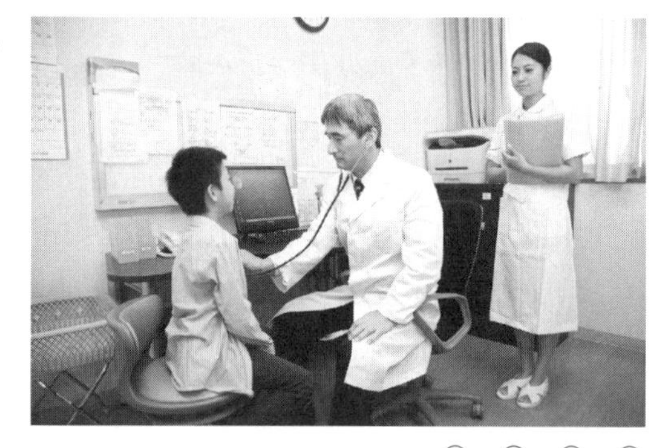

Ⓐ Ⓑ Ⓒ Ⓓ

3.

Ⓐ Ⓑ Ⓒ Ⓓ

Part 1

対処法② 人が写っていたら特徴と持ち物と行動に着目

人が写っているときは男女、職業、服装、持ち物、行動など一瞬で見ないといけない。また、日頃から、特徴・持ち物・行動に関する英語をしっかりと身に付けておくこと。

Part 2 応答問題

Phase 1 Listen, fill in the blank and choose the best response. CD 2-17、18

4. Is the hospital (   ) on weekends?
(A) I'm afraid it's (   ) away.
(B) It's open Monday (   ) Friday.
(C) The patient was (   ) to the hospital.

5. Did you find aromatherapy effective as a (   ) for your symptoms?
(A) I've learned (   ) oil is used for it.
(B) It is one of the interesting (   ).
(C) I'm afraid (   ).

Phase 2 CD 2-19、20、21、22

6. Mark your answer on your answer sheet. Ⓐ Ⓑ Ⓒ

7. Mark your answer on your answer sheet. Ⓐ Ⓑ Ⓒ

8. Mark your answer on your answer sheet. Ⓐ Ⓑ Ⓒ

9. Mark your answer on your answer sheet. Ⓐ Ⓑ Ⓒ

Part 3 会話問題

Phase 1 Choose the better word that suits the blank.

(a) I'd like to have a (through / thorough) medical examination.
(b) An unexpected problem (hopped / popped) up during the discussion.
(c) College students should (sit / stand) on their own feet.
(d) I can't (afford / affect) to buy that kind of imported luxury car.

Phase 2

10. What's wrong with Sam?
(A) He has heart problems.
(B) He has intestinal bleeding.
(C) His stomach is acting up.
(D) His liver is no good.

11. Why does Lucy recommend Sam have another examination?
(A) Because his blood pressure is abnormal.
(B) Because he is overweight.
(C) Because he works too hard.
(D) Because cancer runs in his family.

12. How long will it take for the speakers' children to complete college?
(A) A few weeks
(B) Less than five years
(C) Over five years
(D) A couple of months

Part 4 説明文問題

Phase 1 Fill in the blank with the most appropriate word.

(a) Let me introduce you ( ) Mr. Adams, the president of the company.
(b) She is very popular among young people as ( ) as elderly people.
(c) Doing something ( ) cooperation with others is very important.
(d) Please join me ( ) a warm round of applause to welcome Dr. Anderson.

Phase 2

2-25、26

13. Where is the talk most likely taking place?
(A) A medical equipment company
(B) A research institute in Europe
(C) An academic conference hall
(D) A college library

14. What part of the body does Dr. Cooper specialize in?
(A) Heart
(B) Brain
(C) Stomach
(D) Lungs

15. With whom did Dr. Cooper collaborate to develop a new medical device?
(A) A brain surgeon
(B) A medical reporter
(C) His hospital staff
(D) Some engineers

語彙チェック **症状や病名の英語に注意**

比較的重要なものだけを挙げると・・・
headache（頭痛）、backache（腰痛）、stomachache（腹痛）
high blood pressure（高血圧）、obesity（肥満）、cough（咳）、fever（熱）
pneumonia（肺炎）、gastric ulcer（胃潰瘍）、diabetes（糖尿病）
allergy（アレルギー）、depressive condition（うつ状態）

READING SECTION

Part 5 短文穴埋問題

Phase 1 Choose the better word or phrase that suits the blank.

1. Considering the way Mary looks at him, John thinks that Mary likes (him / himself).
2. In the past, doctors never talked about informed consent, but now they tell us about (anything / nothing) else.
3. The patient has two sons who are being hospitalized: one is in Tokyo, (another / the other) being in Yokohama.

Phase 2

4. There are no bandages on the shelf, but I'm sure ------- are in stock.
(A) any
(B) each
(C) none
(D) some

5. Everyone who wants to have ------- examined in this hospital is supposed to bring a referral from his family doctor.
(A) he
(B) his
(C) him
(D) himself

6. ------- doctor is in charge of the operation in the surgery room.
(A) Another
(B) The rest
(C) Other
(D) Certain

7. Because I don't have a thermometer, I need to get ------- very soon.
(A) any
(B) it
(C) one
(D) that

文法チェック **代名詞**

●重要法則 ··· 再帰代名詞 (oneself) や相互代名詞 (each other や one another) は同じ節内に先行詞（＝その代名詞が指している名詞）が存在しないといけない。

⇒ ○ They saw the two looking at each other. [each other の先行詞は the two]
（彼らは 2 人がお互いに見つめ合っているのを見た）
× He thinks she loves himself. [himself の先行詞が節を超えて he となる]
（彼は彼女が自分自身のことを好きだと思っている）
○ He thinks himself to be loved by her. [先行詞は節を超えず he である]

●重要法則 ··· 人称代名詞 (I, we, you, he, she, it, they···) は、先行詞が同一節内に存在してはならない。

⇒○ She hit her. [her の先行詞は she でない→ she と her は別の人物]
○ He thinks she loves him. この文は 2 つに曖昧。
(a) him の先行詞が he の場合、「彼は彼女が自分のことを愛している」の意味
(b) him の先行詞が he でない場合、「彼は彼女が別の彼を愛している」の意味
注 :「節の外 (= 例えば主文) に存在しなければならない」ではない。だから、先行詞が文中にない [(b) 参照] 場合もある。

Part 6 長文穴埋問題

Phase 1 **Choose the best word that suits the blank.**

(a) He will come back from his trip (at / on / in) the morning of the third.
(b) She can concentrate (on / in / with) her study of business administration.
(c) I have to lose (weigh / weighs / weight) because my doctor says I'm obese.
(d) I kind of feel that my (eye cite / eye site / eyesight) is declining these days.

Phase 2

Notice

There will be a health check on the morning of September 10. The medical examination will be conducted in Conference Room 3 on the eighth -------- (8.) . After finishing the checkup, you should go down to the X-ray trailer -------- (9.) in front of our building.

The procedures in Conference Room 3 will concentrate on the following: height, weight, blood pressure, pulse, eyesight, auditory ability, and urine.

-------- (10.) stomach examinations will be performed, you must not eat breakfast on the inspection day. -------- (11.) . Every employee should take this opportunity to receive a medical checkup.

8. (A) case (B) floor (C) line (D) trip

9. (A) driven (B) stopped (C) parked (D) rented

10. (A) Since (B) Though (C) After (D) Unless

11. (A) Otherwise, it would be necessary for you to drink a glass of water.
(B) Nevertheless, you should eat breakfast on the inspection day.
(C) However, it is okay for you to drink a glass of water.
(D) Accordingly, you will be allowed to eat breakfast on the same day.

語法チェック 食事と不定冠詞

習慣的な食事は無冠詞となる。
breakfast（朝食）、brunch（遅い朝食 [昼食と兼用]）、lunch（昼食）
dinner（夕食）、supper（比較的軽い夕食 [昼に dinner を取った場合]）
習慣的でない「夜食」は不定冠詞が付く。
a night meal [=a midnight snack]（夜食）
※ supper を「夜食」の意味で用いる場合があり、その場合は不定冠詞が付く。
→ I ate a supper of noodles.（夜食に麺類を食べた）

Part 7 読解問題

Phase 1 Choose the best word that suits the blank.

(a) The doctor (diagnosed / diagrammed / dialyzed) his illness as tuberculosis.
(b) Human (intelligent / intelligence / intelligently) might be surpassed by AI.
(c) The company managed to avoid (go / going / gone) bankrupt.
(d) The economist will (analyze / analysis / analytic) the current economic situation.
(e) The general practitioner may (prescription / prescriptive / prescribe) antibiotics.

Phase 2

Artificial intelligence system learns diagnosis

On Wednesday, a team of researchers from the Cambridge General Hospital (CGH) Department of Respiratory Illness has developed a system using artificial intelligence to diagnose and classify lung related diseases.

The system makes a precise decision from relatively limited image datasets. While false diagnosis rate of tuberculosis by medical specialists is approximately 11 percent, misdiagnosis rate by artificial intelligence is only 2.5 percent. As artificial intelligence diagnoses cases, it will accumulate datasets automatically. Once big datasets become available, it will rarely misdiagnose.

Machine learning, the process by which computers analyze data, identifies patterns of images without the involvement of human programmers. In other words, computers teach themselves and get smarter as they deal with more patients.

In order to increase accuracy, CGH has trained the artificial intelligence. Specialists used more than 300,000 images for training. Unlike human brains, AI memorizes all images by extracting features with its image analysis systems.

In collaboration with specialists in CGH, artificial intelligence assists in diagnosing patients. It will not be long before artificial intelligence becomes the physician in charge of your respiratory diseases. CGH says artificial intelligence will not only diagnose but also be able to properly prescribe medication eventually.

The healthcare sector is increasingly adopting artificial intelligence. It can be regarded as practically faultless. Artificial intelligence diagnoses more accurately, works around the clock without complaints, and curbs labor costs; however, it might have algorithmic biases or make unethical decisions. Even with these disadvantages, artificial intelligence in healthcare will be indispensable to all of us.

12. Which is the correct description of artificial intelligence?
(A) Specialists diagnose tuberculosis more precisely than AI.
(B) AI's incorrect diagnosis rate is approximately 11 percent.
(C) It will take AI many years to replace doctors in charge of respiratory diseases.
(D) Big datasets will allow AI to diagnose more precisely.

13. What is implied about machine learning?
(A) It badly needs human programmers.
(B) It becomes smarter even if it deals with fewer patients.
(C) It learns by itself without any human help.
(D) It shows the correct diagnosis rate as only 2.5 percent at present.

14. How has the AI been trained to enhance precision?
(A) AI is exposed to a large number of images so that it will memorize them.
(B) AI is revised so that its unethical decisions can be made useful.
(C) AI is made to work around the clock without making any complaints.
(D) AI is programmed to avoid prescribing medication as much as possible.

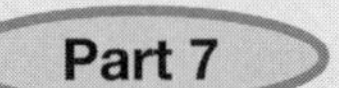

対処法 ④ パラグラフの最初の文に着目する

パラグラフの最初の文が、そのパラグラフをまとめるキーセンテンスであることが多いので、最初の文に着目する。設問を読んで、どのパラグラフを見れば良いかをチェックする。このチェックは、先にキーセンテンスに着目しているとスムーズに済ませることができる。

UNIT 10

Events and Performances

PRE-TOEIC SECTION

Vocabulary Check

次の (1) から (10) の英単語が当てはまる英文を下の (a) ～ (j) から選びなさい。

(1) alternative (　　)　**(2)** apology (　　)　**(3)** assembly (　　)
(4) exclusive (　　)　**(5)** exhibit (　　)　**(6)** explore (　　)
(7) informative (　　)　**(8)** proceed (　　)　**(9)** sauce (　　)
(10) supervisor (　　)

(a) We are going to (　　) various kinds of Buddhist statues in Japan.
(b) The annual conference will take place at an (　　) hall I told you about.
(c) Would it be possible for us to (　　) to the next item on the agenda?
(d) Since the original idea is problematic, I have to figure out an (　　) plan.
(e) This book is both (　　) and interesting, so I recommend you read it.
(f) The newly appointed (　　) often asks me to do odd jobs.
(g) This is the room for the (　　) use of women, so it is safe.
(h) I caused you many troubles. Please accept my sincere (　　).
(i) Teriyaki can be translated as grilling with soy (　　) and sugar.
(j) Medical researchers (　　) every possibility for the treatment of cancer.

TOEIC 語彙と語法 10　**形が似ている重要単語**

① flight（飛行便）、fright（恐怖）、freight（船荷、貨物運送料）
② staff（職員）、stuff（詰め物）、stiff（硬い、[肩などが]凝った）
③ course（コース）、coarse（荒い）、cause（原因、主義、～運動）
④ crash（衝突[する]）、crush（押し潰す）、clash（[意見の]衝突）
⑤ vain（無駄）、vane（風向計）、vein（静脈、葉脈、鉱脈、～の気味）
⑥ pair（ペア）、pear（梨）、pare（[刃物で]皮をむく、[費用を]削減する）
⑦ sauce（[調味料の]ソース）、source（情報源）、souse（塩水、酒宴）
⑧ sour（すっぱい）、sore（痛い）、soar（舞い上がる、暴騰する）

LISTENING SECTION

Part 1 写真描写問題

Phase 1 Listen to the following statements and fill in the blanks.

2-27

1.

Ⓐ Ⓑ Ⓒ Ⓓ

(A) They are all in the ( ) hall of a hotel.

(B) ( ) the people are pine trees.

(C) There are more ( ) than men here.

(D) People are attending a ribbon-cutting ( ).

Phase 2 2-28、29

2.

Ⓐ Ⓑ Ⓒ Ⓓ

3.

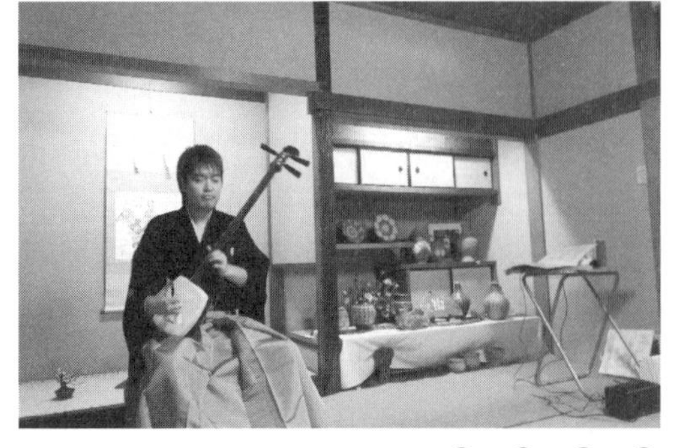

Ⓐ Ⓑ Ⓒ Ⓓ

語法チェック 「場所を表す副詞句＋存在動詞＋主語」の形

Behind the counter are some staff.（カウンターの向こう側に職員がいる）
Over there stands a large house.（向こうに建っているのは大きな家だ）

Part 2 応答問題

Phase 1 Listen, fill in the blank and choose the best response.

CD 2-30、31

4. Will the special (　　　　　　　) be given in Room A or B?
(A) Is she the (　　　　　　　)?
(B) Take a look at the (　　　　　　　).
(C) I'm (　　　　　　　) forward to it.

5. Is the exhibition booth on the third or fourth (　　　　　　　)?
(A) Take the (　　　　　　　) over there.
(B) The exhibition (　　　　　　　) three days.
(C) Neither. It's in the (　　　　　　　).

Phase 2

CD 2-32、33、34、35

6. Mark your answer on your answer sheet. Ⓐ Ⓑ Ⓒ

7. Mark your answer on your answer sheet. Ⓐ Ⓑ Ⓒ

8. Mark your answer on your answer sheet. Ⓐ Ⓑ Ⓒ

9. Mark your answer on your answer sheet. Ⓐ Ⓑ Ⓒ

Part 3 会話問題

Phase 1 Choose the better word that suits the blank.

(a) It's been a long time since I saw you (least / last).
(b) I have been working as a journalist (from / since) I was 25.
(c) John came to be on good (times / terms) with Mary.
(d) I feel quite (frustrated / frustrating) with my job almost every day.

Phase 2

10. What is the woman's present occupation?
(A) An engineer
(B) An editor
(C) A journalist
(D) A taxi driver

11. Why did the man change his job?
(A) He likes driving very much.
(B) He didn't get along well with his boss.
(C) His job made him tired.
(D) He found a less frustrating job.

12. When did the woman quit her company?
(A) At the age of 18
(B) About three months ago
(C) Last March
(D) The last time she met Jack

語彙チェック 「概略」の表現

(a)「概要」: a summary、an outline、a resume（論文など）、a rough sketch
(b)「ほとんど」: almost、practically（実質的に）、in most cases（たいてい）
(c)「大雑把に言って」: roughly、broadly (speaking)、in (rough) outline
(d)「〜の概略を示す」: give an outline of 〜、give the gist of 〜、give a general idea of 〜
summarize 〜、make a summary of 〜、skeletonize 〜 [やや硬い表現]

Part 4 説明文問題

Phase 1 Fill in the blank with the most appropriate word.

(a) First of (   ), let me give you the outline of my presentation.
(b) Would you tell me about what you are interested (   )?
(c) (   ) series of experiments were performed to prove the theory.
(d) I wonder when such an interesting festival will (   ) place.

Phase 2

CD 2-38、39

13. Who most likely are the listeners?
(A) Security guards
(B) Company employees
(C) Human resources staff
(D) College seniors

14. What are the listeners asked to do first?
(A) Contact a personnel director
(B) Find a booth they want
(C) Show their ID
(D) Apply for a written test

15. What will the listeners receive if they meet with personnel department staff?
(A) An entry sheet
(B) Company information
(C) A series of interviews
(D) several resumes

READING SECTION

Part 5 短文穴埋問題

Phase 1 Choose the better word that suits the blank.

1. (Although / Because) the artist gave an impressive performance, the audience gave her a standing ovation.
2. I would appreciate it (if / when) you could be a panelist at the symposium.
3. The speaker gave an informative presentation; (however / moreover), his delivery was not as impressive as the content.

Phase 2

4. ------- it opened, the theme park has drawn a record-breaking turnout due to its flashy advertisements about a wide variety of attractions.
(A) As (B) When (C) Even though (D) Ever since

5. The annual exposition met with great success, ------- world-famous exhibitors participated to showcase their state-of-the-art products.
(A) although (B) as (C) if (D) once

6. The distinguished lecturer gave an insightful speech; -------, the auditorium was not packed to capacity due to the stormy weather.
(A) furthermore (B) nevertheless (C) otherwise (D) therefore

7. ------- an increasing number of people are interested in newer smartphones, the international exhibition on next-generation smartphones is attracting a large audience.
(A) Although (B) Even if (C) Now that (D) Once

文法チェック **接続詞と接続副詞**

●重要法則・・・接続詞には等位接続詞と従位接続詞の２種類があり、語順に注意する。

	等位接続詞	従位接続詞	意味
順接	S1 and S2	Because S1, S2 = S2 because S1	S1 だから S2
逆接	S1 but S2	Though S1, S2 = S2 though S1	S1 だけれど S2

●重要法則・・・接続副詞の位置は３種類ある。（意味は全て「S1 だから / だけれど S2」）

(a) S1; therefore, S2（順接） / S1; however, S2（逆接）

(b) S1. Therefore, S2（順接） / S1. However, S2（逆接）

(c) S1. ・・・, therefore, ・・・（順接） / S1. ・・・, however, ・・・（逆接）
（下線部 ・・・, therefore, ・・・ = S2 / ・・・, however, ・・・ = S2）

Part 6 長文穴埋問題

Phase 1 Choose the best word or phrase that suits the blank.

(a) We would like to hold (three-days / three-day / a three-day) event in autumn.

(b) Our boss tells me that (either / both / nor) you or I am in the wrong.

(c) I am emailing to (acquire / inquire / require) if it is possible to book the hall.

(d) We need a hall that accommodates (most / the most / at most) 100 people.

Phase 2

Dear Sir or Madam.

I work at the Event Planning Department of a manufacturing company in Tokyo. We are planning to hold a two-day event in May next year.

The date is --------(8.) , but the event's first day should be either on Monday or Tuesday, and the meetings will be held from 10 a.m. to 5 p.m. on both days.

I am writing to inquire if it is --------(9.) to hold our event at one of your assembly halls.

We need a large meeting room that will accommodate at most 40 people.

We need a light meal containing coffee, juice, sandwiches, or something else appropriate. We --------(10.) need a projector.

--------(11.) .

Best regards.

8. (A) TBC (B) TBD
(C) IMO (D) TIA

9. (A) able (B) possible
(C) available (D) ready

10. (A) also (B) too
(C) another (D) again

11. (A) We just want to ask you what kind of projector you need for the event.
(B) I am sure you will be satisfied with our facility if you use it this time.
(C) May I ask you about what you really need for the event you are planning?
(D) Could you let me know about the availability of the rooms and rental fees?

語法チェック **another と other は数詞の位置と意味が微妙に異なる**

another three days（もう 3 日間）[=three more days]
three other days（他の 3 日間）
the other three days（残りの 3 日間）

Part 7 読解問題

Phase 1 Choose the best word that suits the blank.

(a) I apologize (to / for / of) being late.
(b) The journalist contributed an essay (with / to / in) the newspaper.
(c) One of my colleagues is suffering (from / of / in) a stomachache.
(d) Admission is free (of / from / in) charge.
(e) Why not come along (on / for / with) me to my office?

Phase 2

e-mail

From: Ethan Franklin
To: Victoria Erikson
Date: January 11
Subject: Apology and a new offer

Dear Victoria Erikson,
The International Agriculture Trade Fair last year was a huge success. We are hoping for an even greater success this year. We appreciate your contribution to the planning and preparation for the fair so far.

I'm afraid that the booth you booked for exhibiting poultry products has become unavailable because of a leaking roof, resulting from Hurricane Nina, which hit last year. Although the event can be held in the hall, some places in Hall C (where your booth is) are suffering from water leakage and cannot be used.

We have explored some alternatives and finally reached the conclusion that we can offer you a booth free of charge in Hall B. Your booth in Hall B is twice as big as the booth you booked. In addition, the booth we will book for you faces a busy aisle. This is an exclusive offer for you.

On behalf of Thompson Planning LLC, I do apologize to you for the inconvenience. It would be great if you could accept our alternative offer.
Sincerely yours,
Ethan Franklin
Thompson Planning LLC

Dear Ethan Franklin,
Thank you for letting us know about the situation, and I appreciate your generous offer. However, I'm afraid to say that we must decline your kind offer because our products are closely related to the products which both neighboring booths offer.

I believe that working closely together with a seasoned flour company and a barbecue sauce company is advantageous. Therefore, it doesn't make any sense if our booth is relocated alone to Hall B. I would be happy to accept your offer if you could consider relocating both of our neighbors' booths along with mine. Of course, we don't mind paying the full fee.

Thank you for your reconsideration and I would really appreciate your understanding.

Best regards,
Victoria Erikson
West Virginia Farm Products Co., Ltd.

12. Why did Ethan Franklin send the e-mail?
(A) To make a full apology for past inconvenience
(B) To offer an apology on behalf of West Virginia Farm Products
(C) To express an apology and make a special offer
(D) To apologize for the storm damage

13. What is the problem in Hall C?
(A) A security leak (B) Small size
(C) A plumbing failure (D) Hurricane damage

14. Which of the following is NOT mentioned as an alternative offer?
(A) A more spacious booth than the one previously booked
(B) A booth more likely to be exposed to public
(C) New drainage for the roof
(D) A free replacement booth

15. The word "decline" in paragraph 1, line 2, in the second e-mail, is closest in meaning to
(A) reduce (B) refuse (C) refute (D) reclaim

16. What kind of food would most likely appeal to people visiting the booths of Victoria and its neighbors?

(A) Deep fried chicken with sauce (B) Barbecued pork
(C) Grilled steak with sauce (D) Beef stroganoff

語彙チェック **否定辞が違えば、微妙に意味や語形が異なる**

(a) unlike（[前] ～と異なり）と dislike（[動] ～が嫌いだ）
(b) unable（[形] できない）と disable（[動] 不可能にする）と inability（[名] 無力）
(c) unused（[形] 使用されていない）と disuse（[名] 不使用）と misuse（[名･動] 誤用 [する]）
(d) uninterested（興味がない）と disinterested（私心のない、公平な、無関心の）
(e) immoral（不道徳な）と amoral（道徳とは無関係の、道徳観念のない）
(f) unbelievable（信じられない）と incredible（信じられない）[in…ible の形]
(g) uneatable（食べることができない）と inedible（食用でない）
※ edible（食用）の食材でも腐っていたら uneatable である。

UNIT 11

College

PRE-TOEIC SECTION

Vocabulary Check

次の (1) から (10) の英単語が当てはまる英文を下の (a) ～ (j) から選びなさい。

(1) candidate ( )
(2) command ( )
(3) concern ( )
(4) enrollment ( )
(5) keynote ( )
(6) prestigious ( )
(7) preventive ( )
(8) proficiency ( )
(9) prospective ( )
(10) sophomore ( )

(a) We will take necessary ( ) measures to avoid the problem.
(b) There has been an increasing number of ( )s for admission to the school.
(c) The student of physics is now a ( ) at the university.
(d) The human resources manager has a good ( ) of English.
(e) She tried to answer all these questions to test her ( ) in English.
(f) Our chief ( ) at the moment is the weather for our athletic festival day.
(g) He is preparing for the entrance exam to a ( ) school.
(h) Our university has a large ( ) of 30,000 students.
(i) Let us introduce all of you to our ( ) speaker, Professor Peter Jones.
(j) A man was formally introduced to a ( ) marriage partner.

TOEIC 語彙と語法 11 **学問名の重要単語**

① geography（地理学）、geometry（幾何学）、geology（地質学）
② physics（物理学）、physiology（生理学）、chemistry（化学）
③ psychology（心理学）、linguistics（言語学）、sociology（社会学）
④ ethics（倫理学）、logic（論理学）、philosophy（哲学）
⑤ mathematics（数学）、economics（経済学）、politics（政治学）
⑥ literature（文学）、mythology（神話学）、history（歴史学）
⑦ ethnology（民族学）、folklore（民俗学）、anthropology（人類学）
⑧ archaeology（考古学）、astronomy（天文学）、astrology（占星術）

LISTENING SECTION

Part 1 写真描写問題

Phase 1 Listen to the following statements and fill in the blanks.

2-40

1.

Ⓐ Ⓑ Ⓒ Ⓓ

(A) The classroom is ( ) of students.

(B) A teacher is hunched ( ) a desk

(C) The man is wearing a ( ) and tie.

(D) The girl is wearing ( ).

Phase 2

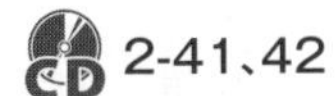
2-41、42

2.

Ⓐ Ⓑ Ⓒ Ⓓ

3.

Ⓐ Ⓑ Ⓒ Ⓓ

Part 2 応答問題

Phase 1 Listen, fill in the blank and choose the best response. CD 2-43、44

4. You're (   ) in law, aren't you?
(A) Yes, I usually eat the meat (   ).
(B) No, I'm an economics (   ).
(C) Yes, I finished (   ) school last year.

5. Let's eat at the (   ), shall we?
(A) Is there any place to eat at this (   )?
(B) That's (   ) as far as I know.
(C) (   ) good.

Phase 2 CD 2-45、46、47、48

6. Mark your answer on your answer sheet. Ⓐ Ⓑ Ⓒ

7. Mark your answer on your answer sheet. Ⓐ Ⓑ Ⓒ

8. Mark your answer on your answer sheet. Ⓐ Ⓑ Ⓒ

9. Mark your answer on your answer sheet. Ⓐ Ⓑ Ⓒ

Part 2 対処法 ③ 否定疑問と付加疑問に注意

英語では、聞き方にこだわらず、肯定なら必ずYes、否定なら必ずNoと答える。
Aren't you a student? / You are a student, aren't you? (学生ではないの？/ ね？)
⇒ Yes. (いいえ、学生です) / No. (はい、学生ではないです)

Part 3 会話問題

Phase 1 Choose the better word or phrase that suits the blank.

(a) The student considered (taking / to take) the geography class.
(b) You have to focus (at / on) something you really want to study.
(c) I make it a rule to work (in / out) daily at the gym near my college.
(d) My professor always says to me, "(Have / Take) your time until you are satisfied."

Phase 2

10. What problem does the man mention?
(A) He is tired of college life.
(B) He is worried about college exams.
(C) He lacks exercise.
(D) He doesn't like his economics class.

11. What does the woman suggest?
(A) That he quit as soon as possible
(B) That he join a gym near his house
(C) That he go to work at nights
(D) That he stick with his original plan

12. What is the man probably going to do?
(A) Request a change of major
(B) Transfer to another apartment
(C) Make more of an effort with his studies
(D) Work out while considering his options

Part 4 説明文問題

Phase 1 Fill the blank with the most appropriate word.

(a) Dr. Jones is an associate professor (　　　　　　) Western Crystal University.
(b) Professor Susan Coleman's presentation will begin (　　　　　　) 2:30 p.m.
(c) She has a large number of books, most of (　　　　　　) are useful for her research.
(d) This area in the city is popular (　　　　　　) its large amusement park.

Phase 2

CD 2-51、52

13. What is the purpose of the announcement?
(A) To discuss syntax in linguistics
(B) To introduce a keynote speaker
(C) To celebrate a 50th anniversary
(D) To explain an event's schedule

14. What does Dr. Salton specialize in?
(A) Syntax　(B) Phonology　(C) Phonetics　(D) Asian history

15. Where is the talk taking place?
(A) A fashionable restaurant　(B) the University of Michigan
(C) A convention center　(D) A popular tourist area

語彙チェック ヨーロッパの主な言語とその言語の話者および国名（英語を除く）

言語名	その英語	話者（1人）	国　名
ドイツ語	German	a German	Germany
オランダ語	Dutch	a Netherlander	the Netherlands
ポーランド語	Polish	a Pole	Poland
スウェーデン語	Swedish	a Swede	Sweden
フィンランド語	Finnish	a Finn	Finland
ノルウェー語	Norwegian	a Norwegian	Norway
デンマーク語	Danish	a Dane	Denmark
フランス語	French	a French(wo)man	France
イタリア語	Italian	an Italian	Italy
スペイン語	Spanish	a Spaniard	Spain
ポルトガル語	Portuguese	a Portuguese	Portugal

READING SECTION

Part 5 短文穴埋問題

Phase 1 Choose the better word or phrase that suits the blank.

1. The prestigious university (was found / was founded) by the famous scholar 100 years ago.
2. The lecture (will give / will be given) in English, with simultaneous interpretation provided.
3. A presentation can be (divided / dividing) into three parts: introduction, body, and conclusion.

Phase 2

4. The professor was pleasantly surprised when he was ------- Deputy of the Faculty at the faculty meeting.
   (A) appoint (B) appointed
   (C) appointed for (D) appointment with

5. Many buildings are currently ------- on campus in order to cope with an expected increase in enrollment in various departments.
   (A) constructing
   (B) constructed
   (C) been constructed
   (D) being constructed

6. The professor adamantly insisted that the deadline for the term paper -------, whatever the situation.
   (A) be met (B) is met
   (C) will be met (D) met

7. The tuition fees of this university have not ------- at all ever since the consumption tax hike five years ago.
   (A) raised (B) be raised
   (C) been raised (D) been raising

文法チェック **受動態と使役**

●重要法則 ･･･ 受動態は SVO → O be+V-ed by S の構造を基本とする。
動作主が存在しないが重要でない場合、by 以外の前置詞を用いる場合が多い。
⇒ be covered with ～（～で覆われる）、be divided into ～（～に分けられる）

●重要法則 ･･･ 使役は使役動詞 (let, make, have) を主として用いる。
let O do ～（O に～させる [するのを許す]（= allow O to do ～）
make O do ～（O に～させる [するのを強要する]（= force O to do ～）
have O do ～（O に～させる、～してもらう [=have ～ done by O]）
注：make のみ、物主語が可能。また、be made to do ～という受動態が可能。

Part 6 長文穴埋問題

Phase 1 Choose the best word or phrase that suits the blank.

(a) I (amounted / belonged / participated) to a glee club when I was a student.
(b) She (attended / attended to / attended on) school regularly last year.
(c) He is thinking of applying (with / to / into) the Finnish language course.
(d) Students are required to produce two credits (merit / value / worth) of written work.

Phase 2

Crystal University's Intercultural Studies Program

We at Crystal University offer our sophomore students belonging to the International Relations Faculty a perfect opportunity for a two-semester -------(8.) to learn Cambodian culture. One year after you enter our university, you may be among the ten students chosen to attend our affiliated Cambodian university: Angkor University. -------(9.) . Prerequisites required to be a candidate for those applying to the two-semester study course at Angkor University are as follows:

#1 GPA should be more than 2.4. after freshman year.

#2 A total of 36 credits should have been earned -------(10.) the second year for all majors.

#3 Must pass an interview test at the end of the first semester of the first year.

#4 Those who have taken two credits worth of a special course in Cambodian culture for students majoring in European, African, Islamic, or Latin American studies at the International Relations Faculty, -------(11.) the above-mentioned 36 credits.

8. (A) cause (B) coarse (C) course (D) corpse

9. (A) It is a national university named Crystal University in Sydney.
(B) It is a private university located in Siem Reap Province, Cambodia.
(C) It is a city university affiliated with Angkor University.
(D) It is a prefectural university established in Hirakata City, Osaka.

10. (A) after (B) before (C) until (D) unless

11. (A) in addition to (B) in spite of (C) in tandem with (D) in contrast to

語法チェック **above-mentioned と mentioned above**

the above-mentioned reasons（先に述べた理由）[前から名詞を修飾]
The reasons mentioned above are…（上に述べた理由は …）[後から名詞を修飾]

Part 7 読解問題

Phase 1 Choose the best word that suits the blank.

(a) Please refrain (of / from / in) smoking on the premises.
(b) There are quite a (many / lot / few) people who lost their jobs due to the sluggish economy.
(c) Our engineers measured the signal (strength / strong / strengthen) .
(d) Mothers (stabilize / sterilize / sterile) feeding bottles in boiling water.
(e) I wonder (weather / that / if) what he says can be true.

Phase 2

e-mail

From: Daniel Thompson
To: Samantha Moore
Date: January 11
Subject: Lifelong Learning Program

Dear Samantha Moore,
My name is Daniel Thompson and I am writing this e-mail on behalf of North Melbourne University Lifelong Learning Center. This e-mail is sent to everyone who registered for our program in the past.

I do apologize to all of you for the long delay in commencement. As you already know, several cases of measles have been confirmed nationwide after the government warned about a potential outbreak last December. We refrained from opening the school just in case. Fortunately, most people have been vaccinated in our region and no cases have been reported.

After taking preventative measures like facility sterilization, mass screening, and individual vaccination history checks, the local health center has allowed us to restart school.

We are pleased to announce that our lifelong learning program is now available. Please register either online or by e-mail. If you have already registered and have an ID, log in and choose the programs you would like to join.

This year, for the first time, we are going to hold an Open School Day. Find out more about our programs and discover how we can support you at this free of charge event. Book your place from the following link and drop in anytime between 10:00 a.m. and 5 p.m. on January 24.

Please don't hesitate to ask me if there is anything that I can help you with. I hope you are thinking about continuing your education and joining our programs. Thank you.

Daniel Thompson
Chief Program Coordinator
North Melbourne University Lifelong Learning Program

From: Samantha Moore
To: Daniel Thompson
Date: January 14
Subject: Re: Lifelong Learning Program

Dear Daniel Thompson,
I am interested in your language program. I learned French as a second language about 20 years ago at college but have forgotten much. I have little confidence in my reading ability, but I do have some degree of confidence in speaking.

According to the brochure attached to the previous e-mail, the language program focuses on conversation. I am just wondering if they teach how to read menus and common signs. My husband and I are planning to visit Paris in May for the first time in ten years.

The ability to try different foods and drinks at various restaurants is my biggest concern about Paris, while my husband shows no interest in it at all. In order to enjoy dining out, reading menus is essential, as well as being able to make conversation with the locals.

Anyway, I would like to know whether the course offered meets my needs. Please inform me of the program details in order for me to decide if the program is suitable for me or not.
Sincerely yours,
Samantha Moore

North Melbourne University Lifelong Learning Programme

Spring Course Offering

567-8900-1779 OR enquiry@ northmelbourneuniversity.edu
Register Online: www.northmelbourneuniversity.edu

ART **Ceramics for beginners**

Learn techniques for sculpting clay by hand as well as glazing. Two consecutive nights' introduction on March 5 and 6, 7:00-9:00 p.m., $120.

WINE **Wine tasting 101 with finger foods**

Learn to taste wine like the experts do and try finger food samples. Thursday, April 7, 6:00-7:00 p.m., $30.

EXERCISE **Yoga for anyone**

Relieve the stress of the day and get in a good workout. Five Fridays, starting March 11, 7:00-9:00 p.m., $80.

PHOTOGRAPHY **Intermediate photography skills**

Designed for digital single-lens reflex users who have a basic understanding of cameras but want to learn more techniques. Four Mondays, starting March 3, 6:00-7:00 p.m., $70.

LANGUAGE **Conversational French**

Make your upcoming trip even better by learning basic words and phrases to use in sightseeing, restaurants, and shopping. Eight Wednesdays, starting February 1 5:00-7:00 p.m., $90.

CHILD CARE EDUCATION **How to work with challenging children**

For specialists who work with challenging children, we'll share strategies and problems, and brainstorm new ideas. Saturday, April 5, 6:00-9:00 p.m., $50.

In addition to the tuition fees stated above, the following fees will be charged.

*Registration fee: $15 (one-time fee for life)

*Insurance: $50 (annually) Every participant in our programs is obliged to register for insurance.

12. What caused the delay in commencement?
(A) A government inspection
(B) An onset of infection
(C) A vaccine shortage
(D) Facility sterilization

13. Who most likely is Samantha Moore?
(A) Daniel Thompson's supervisor
(B) Daniel Thompson's colleague
(C) An administrative officer
(D) A prospective student

14. Which program is intended for professionals?
(A) Photography
(B) Art
(C) Childcare education
(D) Exercise

15. How much must participants with no ID pay for joining the wine program?
(A) $30 (B) $45 (C) $80 (D) $95

16. What is implied about Samantha Moore?
(A) She has never been to Paris.
(B) She has no interest in food and drink in France.
(C) She has limited French proficiency.
(D) She has an excellent command of French.

語彙チェック **アジアの主な言語とその言語の話者および国名（日本語を除く）**

言語名	その英語	話者（不定冠詞）	国　名
中国語	Chinese	a Chinese	China
韓国語	Korean	a Korean	Korea
タイ語	Thai	a Thai	Thailand
ビルマ語	Burmese	a Burmese	Myanmar
カンボジア語	Cambodian	a Cambodian	Cambodia
ラオス語	Laotian	a Laotian	Laos
マレーシア語	Malay	a Malaysian	Malaysia
インドネシア語	Indonesian	an Indonesian	Indonesia
モンゴル語	Mongolian	a Mongolian	Mongolia

UNIT 12

Office

PRE-TOEIC SECTION

Vocabulary Check

次の (1) から (10) の英単語が当てはまる英文を下の (a) ～ (j) から選びなさい。

(1) audit (　　) **(2)** backlog (　　) **(3)** feed (　　)
(4) inform (　　) **(5)** likelihood (　　) **(6)** maintain (　　)
(7) negotiate (　　) **(8)** reminder (　　) **(9)** skyrocket (　　)
(10) triple (　　)

(a) He used to (　　) his dog on scraps.
(b) The policy prompted land prices to (　　) in the capital.
(c) Our company tried to (　　) the original condition.
(d) There is a strong (　　) that the matter will soon be settled.
(e) This is a friendly (　　) about an overdue invoice.
(f) There is something that she wants to (　　) everyone of.
(g) Lucy finished the (　　) of work quite efficiently.
(h) An official examination of a company's financial records is called an (　　).
(i) I will (　　) price cuts with the shop clerk over there.
(j) The sales became about (　　) the amount of those three years ago.

TOEIC 語彙と語法 12　数値の増減を表す表現

① 増える　increase; rise; go up; multiply
② 急増する　increase rapidly/suddenly
③ [物価・株価などが] 急騰する　skyrocket; soar; surge; balloon
④ 減る　decrease; lessen; diminish; dwindle
⑤ 激減する　decrease/drop sharply; fall off sharply
⑥ [物価・株価などが] 急落する　nosedive; plummet; plunge
⑦ 変動する・上下する　fluctuate
⑧ 横ばいである　level off; flat

LISTENING SECTION

Part 1 写真描写問題

Phase 1 Listen to the following statements and fill in the blanks.  2-53

1.

Ⓐ Ⓑ Ⓒ Ⓓ

(A) The man is wearing a ( ) and tie.

(B) The man is ( ) a document.

(C) There is a ( ) of things on the table behind him.

(D) There are ( ) computers on the desk.

Phase 2  1-54、55

2.

Ⓐ Ⓑ Ⓒ Ⓓ

3.

Ⓐ Ⓑ Ⓒ Ⓓ

Part 2 応答問題

Phase 1 Listen, fill in the blank and choose the best response. CD 2-56、57

4. Would you tell your boss to (   ) me this afternoon?
(A) He called me (   ) morning.
(B) I didn't know she called (   ) you.
(C) OK, I (   ).

5. Would you mind telling me the secret (   ) your success?
(A) I don't know. It was just good (   ).
(B) Yes, I do. No (   ).
(C) I was of two (   ) about the final decision.

Phase 2 CD 2-58、59、60、61

6. Mark your answer on your answer sheet. Ⓐ Ⓑ Ⓒ

7. Mark your answer on your answer sheet. Ⓐ Ⓑ Ⓒ

8. Mark your answer on your answer sheet. Ⓐ Ⓑ Ⓒ

9. Mark your answer on your answer sheet. Ⓐ Ⓑ Ⓒ

Part 2 対処法 ④ 疑問詞を含まない疑問文に注意

yes や no が応答とは限らない。特に、Would you mind doing ～？(～していただけませんか？) に注意する。この場合、「はい」に相当する英語は Yes ではない。

Part 3 会話問題

Phase 1 Choose the better word that suits the blank.

(a) Low production cost gives the company an (edge / end) in that industry.
(b) Thousands of letters (swamped / slumped) the newspaper office.
(c) I have a (backpack / backlog) of work to get through.
(d) She succeeded (in / to) reaching the top of the mountain.

Phase 2

10. What kind of industry do the speakers belong to?
(A) Finance
(B) Car
(C) Boating
(D) Law

11. What will Ann most likely do next?
(A) Take a business trip
(B) Negotiate a price
(C) Make a budget
(D) Help write a report

12. What does Nancy mean when she says "Yeah, we are in the same boat."?
(A) They can become advantageous in some respects.
(B) They are as busy as a bee.
(C) They share the same concerns.
(D) They were able to sell many boats this year.

Part 3 対処法 ② 発言の意図を問う問題にはイディオムも頻出

会話特有の表現で、直訳すると意味がよく分からないものについて、What does A mean by …? (A は … で何を意味しているか)の設問が多い。mean の代わりに imply(暗示する)も使用される。普段から会話で使われるイディオムに慣れておこう。

Part 4 説明文問題

Phase 1 Fill the blank with the most appropriate word.

(a) We have to reflect (   ) our past with an eye towards the future.

(b) Our boss should have been more open (   ) change.

(c) I am happy to say that things have never (   ) brighter.

(d) The newly employed manager knew how to keep the staff (   ) line.

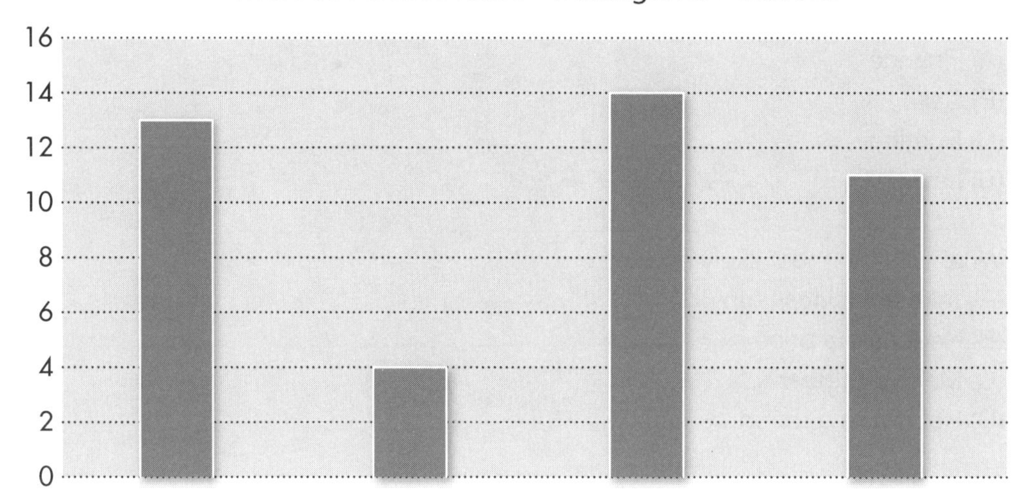

Phase 2

13. What can we say about the speaker?
(A) He is now a conscientious boss that is years ahead of his time.
(B) He admires women a lot more than men.
(C) He oversaw a significant restructuring of management.
(D) He blames men for the lack of success in the past.

14. What is true about the company?
(A) Its shares skyrocketed many years ago.
(B) Things are still not looking brighter.
(C) Its president stepped down to make room for a female.
(D) It experienced positive changes after the merger.

15. Look at the graphic. What is NOT true about the demographic changes in management in the last five years?
(A) A larger number of men hold managerial positions than women.
(B) The number of female managers in 2020 reached 11.
(C) Female managers almost tripled in number recently.
(D) The number of male managers decreased a little.

語彙チェック　quarter の意味と使い方

ビジネスでは、1 年を 4 期に分けて、first quarter（第 1 四半期）、second quarter（第 2 四半期））、third quarter（第 3 四半期）、fourth quarter（第 4 四半期）とすることが多い。

ちなみに、quarter とは「4 分の 1」という基本的な意味があるので、1 時間の 4 分の 1 である「15 分」、1 ドルの 4 分の 1 である「25 セント」の意味もある。

注意すべき用法：　from every quarter = from all quarters（四方八方から）
the Jewish quarter（ユダヤ人街）

READING SECTION

Part 5 短文穴埋問題

Phase 1 Choose the better word or phrase that suits the blank.

1. His dream is to create a book café (which / in which) people sell and buy used books.
2. We know a man (who / whose) first and last names are the same as our professor's.
3. Do you think there is any likelihood (that / what) Lucy will be successful in her new venture?

Phase 2

4. The acting manager is not ------- he used to be; he is now the type of man that is liked by most of his staff.
(A) that (B) what (C) where (D) which

5. Now this is a person ------- I think is very smart; therefore, I want to meet him some day in the near future.
(A) which (B) who (C) whose (D) whom

6. Would you give me some information about a book that you recently bought ------- would be useful for anyone thinking of establishing a company?
(A) which (B) when (C) where (D) whose

7. Something took place ------- my boss, usually very calm, could not have imagined happening.
(A) in which (B) where (C) what (D) which

Part 5　**対処法③ 関係詞の問題は直後と直前（先行詞の確認）が重要**

関係詞の直後に動詞(句)がくると、関係詞は主格、先行詞が人であれば who、物であれば which または that、先行詞がなければ what。

関係詞の直後に主語が来て、その主語を含む文が不完全であれば関係詞は目的格。一方、完全であれば、関係詞は when や where、または<前置詞＋関係詞>となる。

文法チェック　**関係詞**

●重要法則・・・非制限用法：固有名詞が先行詞のとき<コンマ＋関係詞>になる
⇒ I met Tom, who was very kind.（私はトムに会ったが、彼は非常に優しかった）

●重要法則・・・関係詞の省略：関係詞の直後に SV が来ているとき関係詞は省略できる
⇒ I bought the book she told me about.（私は彼女が言っていた本を買った）
This is the book I think is useful.（これは有益だと私が思う本だ）

Part 6 長文穴埋問題

Phase 1 **Choose the best word that suits the blank.**

(a) Did she (change / exchange / vary) her meeting time with you?
(b) The boss was (submitted / suggested / supposed) to come at 10.00 a.m.
(c) If you are (available / convenient / suitable) from 2:00, let me know.
(d) If you fail to reach me, please (leave / remain / rest) a message.

Phase 2

Hello, this is Andy at Universal Technology. I called you this morning to ask -------(8.) to change our meeting time from 1:00 to 2:20. Sorry about this, but our boss, Maria, will have an unexpected visitor from abroad from 1:00 and be with him for -------(9.) . The visitor was supposed to come this morning, but due to a traffic jam, he will arrive later than scheduled. So she decided to meet him at 1:00. If you're available from 2:20, please let me know by phone, rather than by e-mail. -------(10.) . Also, as a -------(11.) , when you arrive at our company's office, please check in at the security desk first to receive a visitor's badge.

8. (A) Andy (B) Maria (C) the visitor (D) you

9. (A) an hour (B) one and a half hours (C) two hours (D) the whole day

10. (A) I am looking forward to meeting him.
(B) I am looking forward to seeing her again.
(C) If I cannot reach you, I will leave a message.
(D) If you cannot reach us, please leave a message.

11. (A) remainder (B) reminder (C) result (D) warning

Part 6 対処法 ③ 慣れている言い回しが答えとは限らない

どうしても知っている表現を見つけると、これが答えだと思ってしまいがち。入念に前後の文を読み、適切な選択肢を選ぶことが大切である。

語法チェック **available と convenient の語法に注意**

I am available on Monday.（月曜日が都合いいです＝月曜日が空いています）
Monday is convenient for me.（月曜日が都合いいです）

Part 7 読解問題

Phase 1 Choose the best word that suits the blank.

(a) He is not a regular student but he is (eligible / suitable / applied) to attend lectures.
(b) I would like to offer a 5-percent discount (at / on / to) the 10 items you have ordered.
(c) Please (permit / allow / forgive) us a few days to send you a new membership card.
(d) The film about sharks will be (seeing / looking / showing) at theaters across the world.
(e) The first (issue / book / magazine) of our journal is full of articles with interesting ideas.

Phase 2

Galapagos Shark Aquarium

Joining Galapagos Shark Aquarium's Quint Club gives you access to all kinds of benefits. On top of unlimited annual admission to the aquarium, all members are eligible to join our daily shark feeding tour once a year for free; moreover, you can enjoy free access to member-only lectures about sharks both online and offline. Membership will give you a 10-percent discount on all purchases made at the aquarium and our online shop.

Register now and get "The Shark Journal," a special edition magazine in commemoration of our founding! Our new annual membership fees are as follows:

- Children $15
  Grades 1-6
- Students $35
  Per person with valid student identification
- Standard $50
  For an individual of any age
- Premium $100
  Per person; complimentary parking, admission to member-only areas, feeding for sharks

*For renewal, 10% discount applicable.
*$5 will be automatically donated from the membership fee for efforts to keep the island environmentally sustainable.

From: Maya Lopez
To: Adrian Harris
Subject: Membership renewal
Date: November 3

Dear Mr. Adrian Harris,

We are very glad that you have decided to renew your premium membership of the Galapagos Shark Aquarium. Your membership fee goes a long way towards helping us maintain current facilities and conduct scientific research on sharks. We have tagged and monitored hundreds of sharks, which helps us maintain a suitable environment for them here.

Please allow us a few days to send you your renewed membership card as well as the first issue of our *Shark Journal*. This issue includes a hand-made shark tooth accessory as a free gift. As we updated our brochure recently, we will enclose the latest version for you. The brochure includes a coupon for a free Shark Burger, which is made of real shark. You can find this and other delicious specialties at our cafeteria.

We'd also like to inform you of a forthcoming film called "No Sharks, No Life." The film will be showing at theaters all over the world and has been translated into 34 languages. We have contributed to the movie and are planning to show it in the aquarium by the end of the year. The film will have showings twice a day at 10 A.M. and 2:30 P.M. and is free for members.

We hope you enjoy your membership and take full advantage of all that the Galapagos Shark Aquarium offers.

Sincerely Yours,
Maya Lopez
Deputy Sales Manager, Galapagos Shark Aquarium

12. What is the main purpose of the notice?
(A) To announce the publication of a scientific magazine
(B) To inform members of lectures about sharks
(C) To promote a new product
(D) To notify members about new membership fees

13. How often are shark feeding tours held?
(A) Every day
(B) Once a week
(C) Once a month
(D) Once a year

14. What is NOT mentioned as a feature of the Galapagos Shark Aquarium?
(A) Shark-themed accessories
(B) Shark-shaped food
(C) Feeding sharks
(D) Screening of shark-themed films

15. How much will Adrian Harris pay for renewing his membership?
(A) $50
(B) $100
(C) $90
(D) $105

16. What does the aquarium want members to do?
(A) Make the most of their benefits
(B) Let other people know about the movie
(C) Try a shark-shaped burger
(D) Donate money for research

対処法 ⑤　職業や業界を問う問題はキーワードを探す

その仕事や業界を暗示するキーワードが、必ず文章内に盛り込まれている。

UNIT 13

Business Trip

PRE-TOEIC SECTION

Vocabulary Check

次の (1) から (10) の英単語が当てはまる英文を下の (a) ～ (j) から選びなさい。

(1) acquainted (　　)　**(2)** aisle (　　)　**(3)** ambitious (　　)
(4) amendment (　　)　**(5)** dispute (　　)　**(6)** observatory (　　)
(7) outsider (　　)　**(8)** sensible (　　)　**(9)** significant (　　)
(10) specific (　　)

(a) He is so (　　) that no one likes him very much.
(b) An (　　)'s comment is invaluable, since lookers-on see more than the players.
(c) There is an astronomical (　　) on the top of the mountain.
(d) It was (　　) of you to refuse the proposal, because it must cost a great deal.
(e) Would you be more (　　) about it? I cannot grasp the whole picture.
(f) The newly employed manager made a (　　) contribution to the company.
(g) "Would you like a window seat?" "Well, I would prefer an (　　) seat."
(h) "I move for an (　　)." "OK, would you tell me about it in detail?"
(i) The manager is in (　　) with his staff about labor problems.
(j) I want to get (　　) with those who are well versed in Japanese culture.

TOEIC 語彙と語法 13　責任者・首長の英語

① 銀行：頭取 (the president of a bank)、支店長 (a branch manager)
　注：銀行家は banker、銀行員は bank clerk (または bank employee)
② 「○○長」の表現
　委員長（the chairperson of a committee)
　自治会長（the president of a residents' association)
　学生自治会長（student council president)
③ 自治体の首長
　知事（governor)、市長（mayor)、町長（town mayor)
　村長（village mayor)、市議会議長（chairperson of a city council)

LISTENING SECTION

Part 1 写真描写問題

Phase 1 Listen to the following statements and fill in the blanks.  2-66

1.

Ⓐ Ⓑ Ⓒ Ⓓ

(A) Everyone is running down the ( ).

(B) The game at the ( ) has finished.

(C) A man is talking ( ) his phone.

(D) There is more than one ( ) of stairs.

Phase 2  2-67、68

2.

Ⓐ Ⓑ Ⓒ Ⓓ

3.

Ⓐ Ⓑ Ⓒ Ⓓ

Part 2 応答問題

Phase 1 Listen, fill in the blank and choose the best response. CD 2-69､70

4. Could you ( ) the lunch on the second day of my itinerary?
(A) All right, ( ) me take care of it.
(B) Who will ( ) the luncheon?
(C) The lunch was ( ).

5. Would you please arrange a meeting with the ( )?
(A) The meeting took ( ) in Room 3.
(B) We are ready to arrange an ( ) tour.
(C) Let me first check whether he's ( ) or not.

Phase 2 CD 2-71､72､73､74

6. Mark your answer on your answer sheet. Ⓐ Ⓑ Ⓒ

7. Mark your answer on your answer sheet. Ⓐ Ⓑ Ⓒ

8. Mark your answer on your answer sheet. Ⓐ Ⓑ Ⓒ

9. Mark your answer on your answer sheet. Ⓐ Ⓑ Ⓒ

Part 3 会話問題

Phase 1 Choose the better word or phrase that suits the blank.

(a) She is ambitious (in a way / in the way).
(b) He was (released / relieved) that his wife was smiling.
(c) After three hours of heated discussion, we got (anywhere / nowhere).
(d) Considering his bad behavior, he will (begin / end) up quitting the company.

Phase 2

10. Where most likely is the conversation taking place?
(A) In an overseas branch
(B) In a major IT firm
(C) In a workplace
(D) At a sales conference

11. Which department do Tim and Jane most likely work in?
(A) Personnel
(B) Accounting
(C) General affairs
(D) Sales

12. What are the speakers mainly talking about?
(A) A headhunter
(B) A new sales manager
(C) The fourth quarter
(D) The former manager's private life

Part 4 説明文問題

Phase 1 Fill in the blank with the most appropriate word.

(a) My computer should be ( ) up to date with new software.
(b) ( ) number of important issues have been discussed at the meeting.
(c) We are ( ) the same page, which can mean we have the same idea.
(d) She is willing to tell you what she thinks about the problem ( ) detail.

Phase 2

CD 2-77、78

13. Why is the speaker going abroad?
(A) To evaluate his company's status
(B) To sell Asian goods
(C) To employ local staff
(D) To solve a labor dispute

14. Where is the speaker going first?
(A) Thailand
(B) Singapore
(C) North America
(D) Europe

15. Which of the following will take place in Thailand?
(A) The closure of some factories
(B) Coordination between Asian branches
(C) Discussion about some important issues
(D) The appointment of a new manager

語彙チェック　綴りの似た単語に注意

(1) aisle 通路 / isle 小島
(2) affect ～ ～に(悪)影響を与える / effect 効果
(3) adapt ～を適合させる、順応する / adopt ～を採用する、養子にする
(4) truck (乗り物の) トラック / track 線路 (Track 3：3番線)、陸上競技
(5) proceed 前進する / precede ～ ～に先んずる (⇔ follow)、～の先に起こる
(6) persecute 迫害する、困らせる / prosecute 起訴する、(着実に) 行う
(7) corporation 会社 / cooperation 協力
(8) collaboration 協力、共同研究 / corroboration 確証

READING SECTION

Part 5 短文穴埋問題

Phase 1 Choose the better word that suits the blank.

1. Take out a travel insurance policy that covers your (all / entire) trip.
2. It would be (sensible / sensitive) of you to book a hotel closest to the airport.
3. Could you check with the airline whether any window seat is (available / convenient) on July 5?

Phase 2

4. I would greatly appreciate it if you could send me a more ------- itinerary for my business trip starting on May 10.
(A) special
(B) specific
(C) specialized
(D) species

5. His presentation disappointed all the managers ------- at the conference.
(A) available
(B) convenient
(C) participatory
(D) present

6. A ------- number of hotels for business travelers are located in the downtown area.
(A) considerable
(B) considerate
(C) considering
(D) considered

7. Here are all your travel expenses, with consumption tax -------.
(A) include
(B) including
(C) included
(D) inclusion

文法チェック **形容詞**

●**重要法則**・・・**限定用法と叙述用法がある。1つの用法のみの形容詞もある(⇒注)。**
名詞を直接修飾する(⇒ a beautiful flower) beautiful は限定用法
補語となる(⇒ The flower is beautiful) beautiful は叙述用法
注:限定用法のみの形容詞⇒ mere(ほんの)、former(前の)、main(主な)
叙述用法のみの形容詞⇒ alive(生きて)、glad(喜んで)、available(入手可能)

●**重要法則**・・・**前置修飾と後置修飾がある。これは分詞の形容詞用法にも当てはまる。**
一般に2語以上のまとまりは後置修飾
前置修飾の例:a large house(大きな家)、a sleeping baby(眠っている赤ん坊)
注:a sleeping car(寝台車) [sleeping は動名詞] (=a car for sleeping)
後置修飾の例:a man afraid of dogs(犬を怖がる男)
a baby sleeping in bed(ベッドで眠っている赤ん坊)
注:性質ではなく一時性を表す形容詞は後置修飾
⇒ the car available(使用可能な車)、the people present(出席者)
参考:a responsible person(信頼できる人)と a person responsible(責任者)

Part 6 長文穴埋問題

Phase 1 Choose the best word that suits the blank.

(a) The cost did not (fall / drop / turn) within the range allowed by the boss.
(b) The hotel is located (at / into / within) a five-minute bus ride of the airport.
(c) There is a very nice shopping (mole / mall / male) near the subway station.
(d) The office on top of the building commands a fine (sight / scene / view) of the city.

Phase 2

Dear, Mr. Adam Roderick.

Thank you for your e-mail.

As for the hotel you will stay at during your trip, I would like to recommend the Kansas Airport Hotel.

They can offer you a single room for two nights on your business trip from August 12th to 14th.

They can prepare rooms which -------(8.) either $150 or $180 per night, which falls within the range you are considering. The difference in cost is due to the room size. Which room would you like?

The reason I recommend this hotel is that it is located within a 5-minute walk of the conference hall; -------(9.) , there is a very nice shopping mall near the hotel.

According to many of their guests, the Sky Lounge on top of the hotel -------(10.) a wonderful view of the city. -------(11.) .

I am looking forward to your reply.

Regards,

Yukio Katagiri

Stardust Tour Company

8. (A) cost (B) spend (C) pay (D) charge

9. (A) however (B) therefore (C) moreover (D) otherwise

10. (A) orders (B) dominates (C) commands (D) governs

11. (A) Are you sure she will enjoy her stay at the hotel?
(B) Is she sure they will enjoy their stay at the hotel?
(C) He is sure you will enjoy your stay at the hotel.
(D) I am sure you will enjoy your stay at the hotel.

Part 7 読解問題

Phase 1 Choose the best word that suits the blank.

(a) We will see how things turn (out / on / off) .
(b) Huge costs were (incur / incurring / incurred) due to his lack of planning.
(c) Nothing is as (costly / cost / costing) as a free gift.
(d) (Of / At / On) behalf of the company, I express our gratitude to you.
(e) Have all your (belong / belongings / belongs) with you.

Phase 2

e-mail

From: Ava Williams
To: Lucas Miller
Date: February 7
Subject: Reimbursement for business trip

Dear Lucas,
I am writing this e-mail to inform you that the discussion regarding the international game show for which I had to travel to Japan turned out to be a huge success. The clients were highly impressed with my presentation and the facts, figures, and future perspective presented by me.

However, all the expenses incurred on the trip were borne by me. As the contract says, your company has promised to bear all costs: travel including air, train, bus and taxi; accommodation; and food. Due to cultural differences, I had to treat some executives to an extravagant dinner in order to have them sign the contract. Since it was a different country and has a different culture, I was compelled to pay the extra cost unexpectedly. I would like to request reimbursement for these unforeseen costs.

I have attached all the necessary documents and details of payments along with this e-mail for your reference. Please process the repayment as soon as possible. I hope I can expect full cooperation from your side.

Yours sincerely,

Ava Williams
Senior Consultant
Manhattan Thomas Consulting LLC.

Hello Ava,

Thank you for your e-mail. On behalf of Smith Amusement & Entertainment Ltd., I appreciate your great contribution to this matter from the bottom of my heart. No one could have achieved the same level of success as you.

Regarding the full reimbursement including the pricey dinner, my supervisor and the manager of our financial department have fully approved. In addition to the full reimbursement of $7,200, we have decided to pay 20 percent as a bonus on top of the $10,000, which is the formerly agreed upon consulting fee.

In accordance with the major amendment of our payment regulations enacted from January 3, all paperwork has been renewed. I'm afraid that documents you attached therefore are invalid. Please fill out all documents attached to this e-mail and send them back to me at your earliest convenience.

Thank you for your understanding and feel free to ask me if you have any questions regarding documentation. The payment will be made two weeks after our financial department receives all required documents. Please remember that in case of insufficient paperwork, the payment will be delayed accordingly.

For your information, our company has introduced a corporate debit card for business trips. As you belong to a subcontracting company, you are qualified to use it. It will dramatically reduce your burden in documentation as well as problems with unexpected expenses. Please let me know three weeks in advance if you would like to take a card with you on your next business trip.

Looking forward to hearing from you soon.

Lucas Miller

Deputy Event Manager
Smith Amusement & Entertainment Ltd.

Dear Lucas,

Thank you for your consideration. Your response is greatly appreciated. I am thoroughly satisfied with the arrangement. Couldn't be better!

I have attached the required documents in a format compliant with your newly-introduced regulations. Although I have thoroughly checked the documents, please let me know if you find something incomplete.

With respect to a corporate debit card, I would like to have one with me for my upcoming business trip to Amsterdam in March. It would be great if you could send any necessary documents for application.

Again, I appreciate your consideration and I will do my best not to let you down.

Sincerely,

Ava Williams
Senior Consultant
Manhattan Thomas Consulting LLC.

12. For what reason did the trip succeed?
(A) Ava's presentation was convincing.
(B) Ava presented impressive figures to Lucas.
(C) Ava spent a lot of money to prepare.
(D) Ava was treated to an extravagant dinner.

13. Which of the following is NOT mentioned as costs covered by the company in the contract?
(A) Taxi fare
(B) Hotel bills
(C) Costs of meals
(D) Tips

14. How much will Ava Williams receive in total?
(A) $7,200
(B) $12,000
(C) $17,200
(D) $19,200

15. Why does Ava William have to fill out a form again?
(A) Because of a typing error
(B) Because of a calculation error
(C) Because of revised regulations
(D) Because of additional costs accrued

16. The sentence "Couldn't be better!" in paragraph 1, line 2, in the third e-mail is closest in meaning to
(A) It's wonderful.
(B) It's worse.
(C) It's catastrophic.
(D) It's expected.

語彙チェック **ee で終わる単語**

(1) employee 従業員 [=employ された人] cf. employer（雇用主）
(2) payee（手形・小切手などの）受取人 [= pay される人] cf. payer（支払人）
(3) addressee 受信人、名宛人 cf. addresser（発信人）
(4) attendee 出席者、参加者
(5) absentee 欠席者、不在投票者

UNIT 14

Sightseeing

PRE-TOEIC SECTION

Vocabulary Check

次の (1) から (10) の英単語が当てはまる英文を下の (a) ～ (j) から選びなさい。

(1) appetizing ( ) **(2)** challenging ( ) **(3)** combine ( )
(4) comply ( ) **(5)** file ( ) **(6)** interfere ( )
(7) pose ( ) **(8)** prohibit ( ) **(9)** scenic ( )
(10) shuttle ( )

(a) A ( ) bus is run from the station to the venue.
(b) A barrage of questions raised by the audience ( )ed with the lecture.
(c) Everything served at this fashionable restaurant looks ( ).
(d) Many countries passed laws to ( ) people from smoking in public places.
(e) The tour conductor is going to ( ) a complaint with the tour company.
(f) It is possible but highly ( ) for me to translate this book into English.
(g) All the tourists attending the tour ( )d for several souvenir pictures.
(h) He is so obstinate that I don't think he is going to ( ) with your request.
(i) I try to make it a rule to ( ) business with pleasure to some degree.
(j) I really want to visit as many ( ) spots as possible in that country.

TOEIC 語彙と語法 14 **旅行関連用語**

① **旅行の表現のいろいろ** ･･･travel（旅行、特に長期間）、trip（短期の旅行）、tour（観光や視察）、journey（長期の旅行、必ずしも帰ってくることを意味しない）、pleasure trip（慰安旅行、[会社の] company trip）、voyage（船旅）、excursion（団体で行う小旅行、遠足）

② **旅行に関連する機関** ･･･tour company（旅行会社）、travel agency（旅行代理店）、the customs（税関）、duty-free shop（免税店）、exchange counter（両替所）、rental car store（レンタカー店）

③ **移動手段のいろいろ** ･･･sightseeing bus（観光バス）、streetcar（路面電車）、cable car（ケーブルカー）、ropeway（ロープウェー）

LISTENING SECTION

Part 1 写真描写問題

Phase 1 Listen to the following statements and fill in the blanks.  2-79

1.

Ⓐ Ⓑ Ⓒ Ⓓ

(A) A woman is ( ) by several people.

(B) A woman is wearing a ( ).

(C) People are walking along the ( ) street.

(D) People are getting ( ) a car.

Phase 2  2-80、81

2.

Ⓐ Ⓑ Ⓒ Ⓓ

3.

Ⓐ Ⓑ Ⓒ Ⓓ

Part 2 応答問題

Phase 1 Listen, fill in the blank and choose the best response. CD 2-82､83

4. Could you tell me (   ) I get to the City Museum?
(A) The museum is very (   ) on Sundays.
(B) Until the (   ) of this month.
(C) I'm a (   ) here myself.

5. Would you take a picture of me (   ) the tower in the background?
(A) I'd like to (   ) a picture of the tower.
(B) Why (   ) just use that selfie stick you've got there?
(C) You took a picture (   ) the sun.

Phase 2 CD 2-84､85､86､87

6. Mark your answer on your answer sheet. Ⓐ Ⓑ Ⓒ

7. Mark your answer on your answer sheet. Ⓐ Ⓑ Ⓒ

8. Mark your answer on your answer sheet. Ⓐ Ⓑ Ⓒ

9. Mark your answer on your answer sheet. Ⓐ Ⓑ Ⓒ

Part 3 会話問題

Phase 1 Choose the better word that suits the blank.

(a) Are you going to stay (by / until) the 10th of November?
(b) She is planning (to / on) enjoying cherry-blossom viewing next week.
(c) The total cost of his business trip may (add / plus) up to 1,650 dollars.
(d) Your whole tour (contains / includes) a complimentary shuttle bus to the hotel.

Phase 2

10. Where is the conversation most likely taking place?
(A) A baseball park
(B) An airport
(C) A travel agency
(D) A hotel

11. What is the man most excited about?
(A) Using a free shuttle bus
(B) Staying at a four-star hotel
(C) Shopping downtown
(D) Watching a baseball game

12. What does the woman suggest the man do?
(A) Cancel his baseball ticket
(B) Deliver the package to her quickly
(C) Downgrade his stay to save money
(D) Take a taxi from the airport

Part 4 説明文問題

Phase 1 Fill in the blank with the most appropriate word.

(a) The event producing committee consists (　　　　　　) 36 members.
(b) Shirakami-sanchi sits (　　　　　　) the border between Akita and Aomori Prefectures.
(c) Todaiji Temple is famous (　　　　　　) its huge seated statue of Buddha Vairocana.
(d) The Gion Festival has been held (　　　　　　) the eighth century in Japan.

Phase 2

13. Who most likely are the listeners?
(A) Horseback riders (B) Boaters (C) Lifeguards (D) Tourists

14. Which falls does the speaker most recommend the listeners see?
(A) American Falls (B) Horseshoe Falls (C) Bridal Veil Falls (D) Niagara Falls

15. What is Niagara Falls' greatest challenge for the future?
(A) To reduce the number of tourists
(B) To increase the flow rate of the American Falls
(C) To keep the area around the falls clean
(D) To balance leisure and industrial uses

語法チェック **increase の使い方**

(1) increase in ～：～が増す
As he walked up the street, the rain increased in force.
（彼が通りを歩くにつれて、雨脚が強くなってきた）
(2) an increase in ～：～の上昇
She is wishing for an increase in wages.（彼女は賃上げを望んでいます）
(3) an increasing number of ～：～が増えてきている
There has been an increasing number of women launching businesses recently.
（最近は起業する女性が増えてきている）
(4) on the increase：増えてきている
Unemployment is on the increase.（失業が増えてきている）

READING SECTION

Part 5 短文穴埋問題

Phase 1 Choose the better word that suits the blank.

1. This shrine is extremely crowded (for / with) many worshippers on New Year's Day.
2. Reserve a seat on a one-day sightseeing bus well (in / on) advance.
3. Look on websites to get detailed information (on / with) scenic sightseeing destinations.

Phase 2

4. This travel coupon is applied only ------- those who have bought it online.
   (A) in (B) on
   (C) to (D) with

5. According to the itinerary, ------- the first day you will visit the world famous City Museum.
   (A) at (B) on
   (C) to (D) with

6. Were you satisfied ------- your stay in the Metropolis yesterday evening?
   (A) at (B) on
   (C) to (D) with

7. ------- your first destination, you will visit the observatory on the 50th floor, which commands a spectacular view of the city and its vicinity.
   (A) At (B) In
   (C) Toward (D) With

文法チェック　前置詞

●重要法則・・・十大基本前置詞の用例に慣れておく。

of：所有の of（legs of a desk）、目的格の of（the gift of a book）など多数の用法。
at：点的な場所と時間・年齢を表す。at a point、at ten（10 時に、10 歳の時）など。
on：線的な場所と日程および接触を表す。on a line、on the third（3 日に）など。
in：面的な場所と時間および空間内を表す。in Japan、in 2020、in a box など。
from：起点・視点・分離・原料を表す。absent from、make wine from grapes など。
to：方向・結果・適合などを表す。rise to wealth（金持ちになる）、agree to など。
for：目的・追求・用途・代用・賛成・原因および不定詞の主語など多数の用法。
into：「中に入り込む」意味から結果・夢中など。I'm into golf.（ゴルフに夢中だ）。
with：同伴・混合・一致などと付帯状況（with O C [O が C の状態で]）の用法。
by：近隣・経由・手段および動作主 (受け身の by)。north by east（東寄りの北）など。

●重要法則・・・名詞化すると前置詞が現れる。＜前置詞＋名詞＞で格を表す。

John gives Mary a book. ⇒ the gift <u>of a book</u> <u>to Mary</u> <u>by John</u>
対格　与格　主格

Part 6 長文穴埋問題

Phase 1 **Choose the best word that suits the blank.**

(a) She usually (abducts / conducts / deducts) tours as a professional guide.
(b) It was hard for me to (carry / hold / deliver) the bag upstairs.
(c) I will (go / take / make) picnicking with my friend if it is fine tomorrow.
(d) He got (at / on / in) his bicycle and went to the nearby 100-yen shop.

Phase 2

Nara Ancient City Tour

On May 8th , we are going to conduct a sightseeing tour of Nara; however, we do more than just ------- (8.) .

First, in the morning, we will visit an old Japanese house and make a Japanese lunch box using traditional Japanese ingredients. We will carry our lunch boxes and go ------- (9.) before midday while enjoying views of the ancient city.

------- (10.) . This is the ideal place to learn about the oldest city in Japan. After lunch, we'll get on our bikes again and ride to a traditional Japanese sweets factory, where we'll sample rice cakes ------- (11.) with sweet bean jam and drink green tea.

Please e-mail us at ancientcapitaltour@crystaltourist.co.jp for more information and reservations.

8. (A) offering (B) sightseeing (C) Nara tour (D) catch deer

9. (A) cycle (B) cycling (C) to cycle (D) cyclist

10. (A) We will eat lunch in the open space neighboring the Ancient Capital Hall.
(B) We are going to eat supper before going to the Ancient Capital Hall.
(C) Before lunch, we will visit one of our most traditional Japanese sweets factories.
(D) After supper, we are going to get on our bikes and visit some famous sites.

11. (A) flashed (B) flushed (C) staffed (D) stuffed

語法チェック **neighbor の形容詞用法と動詞用法**

(1) 形容詞用法：限定用法のみで用いる。
⇒ neighbor countries（近隣諸国）

(2) 動詞用法：自動詞（neighbor on ～）と他動詞（neighbor ～）の2つがある。
neighbor on ～は「～の近くに住んでいる」、neighbor ～は「～に隣接する」
⇒ The post office neighbors the police station.
（郵便局が警察署に隣接している）

Part 7 読解問題

Phase 1 Choose the best word that suits the blank.

(a) The (flight / freight / fright) between New York and Tokyo takes 12 hours.
(b) An (intention / itinerary / intonation) is a detailed plan for a journey.
(c) I'm sorry but we have no (vacancy / vacate / vacant) at present .
(d) An (annex / appendix / affiliate) means a subsidiary building or an addition to a building.
(e) The manager gave (advise / advices / advice) to a sales representative.

語彙チェック **色々な店の英語**

パン屋 bakery / 八百屋 vegetable shop / 肉屋 butcher's store / 魚屋 fish shop /
食料雑貨店 grocery / 薬屋 drugstore / クリーニング店 laundry / 靴屋 shoe store /
仕立屋 tailor's (shop) / 衣料品店 clothing store / 散髪屋 barber (shop) /
美容院 beauty parlor / 本屋 bookstore / 新聞売店 newsstand /
電気屋 appliance store / 家具屋 furniture store / おもちゃ屋 toy store /
花屋 flower shop / 写真屋 photo shop / 眼鏡屋 glasses shop /
文房具店 stationery store / 自動車販売店 auto dealer / 自動車修理工場 garage /
菓子屋 confectionery, candy store, sweet shop / 居酒屋 pub, bar /
託児所 day nursery, day-care center /
老人ホーム elderly nursing home, home for elderly people /
喫茶店 tearoom, coffee shop / 猫カフェ cat café

語法チェック **advice と advise の使い分け**

(1) advice は不可算名詞で「忠告」の意味
⇒ She gave some useful pieces of advice to him.
(彼女は彼にいくつかの有益なアドバイスをした)
(2) advise は「忠告する」という意味の動詞
⇒ You should advise her to be cautious.
(彼女に慎重にするよう忠告すべきです)

Phase 2

From: Elizabeth White
To: Allison Jones
Date: June 8
Subject: Confirmation of your travel arrangements

Dear Allison Jones,
This e-mail is to confirm the preparations that we discussed over the phone this morning. Attached to this e-mail are your itinerary and e-tickets for Pan-Europe Airlines flight 207, leaving Taipei at 1:30 p.m. on Tuesday, December 7, 2020, arriving in Bangkok at 10:45 p.m. via Seoul.
Our tour guide, Ryan Rodriguez, will be there at the airport in Bangkok to meet you. He will be wearing a red jacket and holding a small signboard with your name on it. He will drop you off at the hotel you'll be staying at. As per your request, I haven't booked your return ticket so that you can have flexibility during your stay in Bangkok. Please take a close look at the attached files in order to make sure procedures, fees, and terms and conditions for booking a return ticket are agreeable.
I have reserved a room at a hotel downtown for your five-night stay. I do apologize, but none of the rooms with scenic views were vacant. However, I can assure you that the view from your room is still satisfactory. The hotel also has excellent facilities, such as a huge swimming pool, a gym, restaurants, and so on. These are available 24/7.
As the hotel is directly connected to a large shopping mall, you can walk there in about a minute from the reception floor. A wide range of dining facilities and entertainment facilities are available in the shopping mall. Furthermore, there is a hospital directly to the north of the mall.
I believe that these arrangements will surely meet your requirements. If you have any questions or requests, please feel free to contact me via e-mail. Thank you for choosing Jakarta Tours. We hope you enjoy your holiday!

Have a safe trip!
Sincerely,

Elizabeth White
Travel Agent,
Jakarta Tours Co., Ltd..

<Attached file>

How to Book

Visit Pan-Europe Airlines at www. paneuropeairlines.com and confirm your flight. You will be charged a $50 booking fee on your credit card. After you complete your booking, you will receive a confirmation e-mail with a booking number. Keep the e-mail with you and show it at the check-in counter.

Changes and Cancellations

You are eligible to submit a request for change and/or cancellation a total of two times by e-mail at inquire@paneuropeairlines.com. Other means of changing the status of your flight are not accepted.

In the event that you make any alteration to your booking (cancellation or modification), our standard fee of $75 will be applied as is outlined in our policy. Please bear in mind that changes to name and details including your passport number are not allowed.

If you wish to cancel your booking because you are unable to comply with the passport, visa, and other immigration requirements applicable to your itinerary, the terms and conditions of the airline will apply and we accept no responsibility for any charges incurred.

Refund

All discounted tickets are non-refundable.

*Your ticket is NOT a discounted ticket but a standard one. Ticket fees will be refunded with a $100 refund commission charge.

Hello Elizabeth White,

Thank you for sending me the itinerary and the e-ticket. The plan is perfect, and I am very happy with it.

As I said on the phone, I would like to have your tour guide with me while staying in Bangkok. I have some concerns about the tour guide, though. My biggest concern is whether tipping him is customary in Thailand or not. Another concern is that I worry I'll disturb him if I make him wait while I am shopping, which always takes me a considerable amount of time.

Moreover, I am wondering if I should pay for his meals. I will meet some of my old friends and may have long chats with them over dinner. His presence at dinner may interfere with our conversation but I would feel guilty if I made him wait outside without dinner. As I definitely need his help both in restaurants and returning to the hotel, I would like him to be with me as much as possible. I would appreciate it if you could advise me in this.

Regards,
Allison Jones

12. Where will flight 207 land initially?
(A) Taipei
(B) Seoul
(C) Bangkok
(D) Jakarta

13. Which of the following is NOT mentioned in the first e-mail?
(A) Airport pickup
(B) Hotel reservation
(C) Restaurants
(D) Local festivals

14. According to terms and conditions, what should the customer do in case of cancellation?
(A) Make another reservation
(B) Visit an airline counter
(C) Make a phone call to the airline
(D) Send an e-mail to a designated address

15. Which statement can be inferred from the terms and conditions?

(A) Passengers can file a claim for any damage at the counter.

(B) All passengers are eligible to get a refund in case of cancellation.

(C) A third alteration or cancellation will be not accepted.

(D) Passengers who booked online do not need to use the check-in counter.

16. What is one of Allison Jones's primary concerns?

(A) Extended conversation with friends

(B) Inability to comply with her passport

(C) Whether paying gratuities is expected or not

(D) Disturbing her guide by talking too much to him

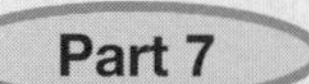

対処法 ⑥　設問や選択肢内で本文の単語を言い換えていることが多い

「予約する」は book と reserve、「心付け」は tip と gratuities など、同義の単語を普段から確認しておくことが重要である。

LINGUAPORTA

リンガポルタのご案内

リンガポルタ連動テキストをご購入の学生さんは、
「リンガポルタ」を無料でご利用いただけます！

本テキストで学習していただく内容に準拠した問題を、オンライン学習システム「リンガポルタ」で学習していただくことができます。PCだけでなく、スマートフォンやタブレットでも学習できます。単語や文法、リスニング力などをよりしっかり身に付けていただくため、ぜひ積極的に活用してください。

リンガポルタの利用にはアカウントとアクセスコードの登録が必要です。登録方法については下記ページにアクセスしてください。

https://www.seibido.co.jp/linguaporta/register.html

本テキスト「TOEIC® L&R TEST オールラウンド演習」のアクセスコードは下記です。

7213-2044-1231-0365-0003-0066-Y4Z8-S45V

・リンガポルタの学習機能（画像はサンプルです。また、すべてのテキストに以下の4つの機能が用意されているわけではありません）

●多肢選択

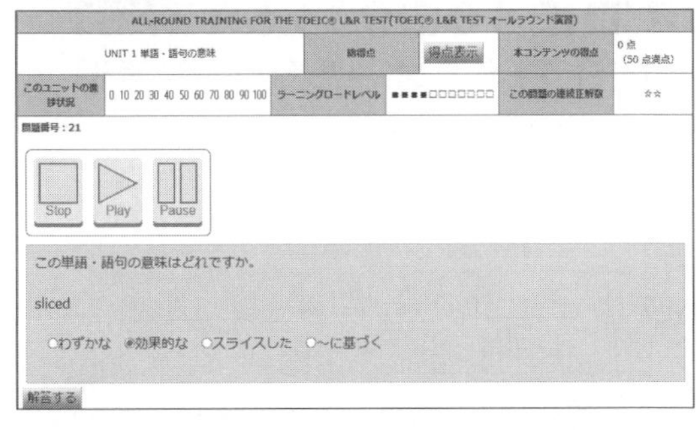

●空所補充（音声を使っての聞き取り問題も可能）

ALL-ROUND TRAINING FOR THE TOEIC® L&R TEST(TOEIC® L&R TEST オールラウンド演習)
UNIT 1 音声を聞いて書き取り
問題番号：8
音声を聞いて、空所部分の英文を書き取りなさい。
I asked Beth to organize the reception because she is most capacity person.
解答する

●単語並びかえ（マウスや手で単語を移動）

ALL-ROUND TRAINING FOR THE TOEIC® L&R TEST(TOEIC® L&R TEST オールラウンド演習)
UNIT 1 単語並び替え
問題番号：9
日本文に合う英文になるように、単語を黒いラインの上に並べなさい。
我々の徹底した準備の結果として、その会議は滞りなく進行した。
As a result of / our / thorough / preparation, / the conference / without a hitch. / proceeded
解答する　クリア

●マッチング（マウスや手で単語を移動）

TOEIC(R)テストに役立つビジネス英単語(Target on Business and the TOEIC(R) Test Vocabulary)
(0101～0150)マッチング
問題番号：2
Match the following English with its Japanese definition.
content / custom / database / court / cost
データベース / 習慣 / 損失 / 趣旨 / 法廷
解答する　リセット

TEXT PRODUCTION STAFF

edited by	編集
Taiichi Sano	佐野 泰一
cover design by	表紙デザイン
Nobuyoshi Fujino	藤野 伸芳
text design by	本文デザイン
ALIUS	アリウス

CD PRODUCTION STAFF

narrated by	吹き込み者
Howard Colefield (AmE)	ハワード・コールフィールド（アメリカ英語）
Karen Haedrich (AmE)	カレン・ヘドリック（アメリカ英語）
Guy Perryman (BrE)	ガイ・ペリマン（イギリス英語）
Neil Demaere (CnE)	ネイル・デマエレ（カナダ英語）
Sarah Greaves (AusE)	サラ・グリーブス（オーストラリア英語）

ALL-ROUND TRAINING FOR THE TOEIC® L&R TEST
TOEIC® LISTENING AND READING TEST オールラウンド演習

2020年1月20日　初版発行
2024年3月5日　第6刷発行

編著者　石井 隆之　平田 千夏　松村 優子
　　　　山口 修　岩田 雅彦　Joe Ciunci

発行者　佐野 英一郎

発行所　株式会社 成美堂
〒101-0052　東京都千代田区神田小川町3-22
TEL 03-3291-2261　FAX 03-3293-5490
https://www.seibido.co.jp

印刷・製本　三美印刷（株）

ISBN 978-4-7919-7213-5　　Printed in Japan